Book of One :-)

Volume 1

Lightworker's Log

SAM

Copyright © 2013 SAM/Lightworker's Log

All rights reserved.

ISBN 978-1-939890-04-7

Brief quotations embodied in critical articles and reviews allowed. Include the book's title, author's name, and the Lightworker's Log website (LightworkersLog.com) as sources of further information. Contact the author via the above website to comment, for written permission regarding longer excerpts, or to otherwise use or reproduce this book.

Views expressed in this book are solely those of the author's perception at the time of writing. Channeled material flowed through the author from 2006 to March 2012. The author makes no warranties as to the accuracy, completeness, timeliness, or usefulness of this information. The author's intent is only to share information to help you in your quest for emotional and spiritual well-being. You are solely responsible if you use any of the information in this book for any purpose.

Because of the dynamic nature of the Internet, Web addresses or links contained in this book may have changed since publication and may no longer be valid.

Lovingly dedicated to everything within and out of this illusion of time and space, with great appreciation for the Light of Truth that lies within to carry all Home to the BEingness of *All That Is*.

Contents

Author's Note	vi
Preface	viii
Book of One :-) Begins in Earnest	1
Glimmers of Light	9
Flashes of True BEing	36
Author's Experiences	98
Tidbits on BEing	129
About the Author	131

LightworkersLog.com

Author's Note

"You can change your perceptions of earth very beyond what you have here."

This message entered my mind upon waking one morning in 2006.

The journey of changing perception varies but altered perception always creates permanent change for everyone because in *Reality* we are One. More help than ever before now flows through the veil of forgetfulness. Since it's impossible to see what we do not believe, sometimes the journey accelerates when loved ones transition to the Otherside. Departed loved ones offer unique opportunities to alter perceptions by speaking to us after physical death. They continue to help us more easily make the transition of the ages.

A New World is emerging quickly. But we must change our perception to experience it fully, for as our perception changes so does our way of experiencing the world. Years of listening to departed loved ones helped me to realize that continually adjusting perceptions and beliefs paves the way to new experiences. Perception builds on the basis of experience so it's helpful to see things from different points of view. We can then choose the point of view that leads us to greater good.

All things are possible with limitless thinking for our thoughts change the circumstances around us. We can master every condition by changing our perception of how we see it because our reactions control what happens in our world. Universal Energy belongs to, and works with, everyone. We

LightworkersLog.com

are a part of this indestructible energy. Once we realize the divinity within we set that energy free to show us we are unlimited in all that is good.

Because our mind is a distribution center for the entire Power-in-Action of the Originating Thought, we can manifest at will. Tuning into that Awesome Power in which we live, and move, and have all BEing makes this possible. Changing perception to more closely align with *It* changes the world we experience. Connecting to *It* allows us to be at peace regardless of what happens around us.

Life improves drastically when we focus on the Oneness of all humanity. Ultimately, we are here to recognize that we are a unique part of Spirit, God, whatever term you choose to name the unerring and perfect one, in which we live, and move, and have all BEing. The *Book of One :-)* helps us to recognize this.

Tapping into that Consciousness in which we live, and move, and have all BEing becomes effortless with practice. This learned behavior frees us from limitation. *Book of One :-)* holds Glimmers of Light, Flashes of True BEing, the author's experience, and Tidbits on BEing. It helps us to tune into the Universal Energy of which we are. I trust you will enjoy reading and contemplating the messages within the *Book of One :-)* as much as I do.

Preface

Life seems often to be a dream; and yet, everything on earth feels so real. Of course, I know it is not. Everything is just a figment of my imagination. Many years passed while thinking about how this earth and its inhabitants came to be. Perhaps I have things figured out now, finally after eons of time, I remember.

The truth is we are lost in a sea of forgetfulness, playing a game called earth life. It is not, nor has it ever been, our intent to stay but just to experience, express, and expand back to *All That Is*. Sometime back, I'm not sure when, we decided to change the game. Allow me to start from what I now perceive as the beginning.

In the beginning there was the Word, yeah, the Word, the Word of One. But putting that aside, there was a black Void of emptiness and fullness, everywhere, including everything. That Pure Consciousness was *All* and still is *All That Is*. It somehow began to expand by thinking, manifesting if you will, parts of *Itself* that wished to create more and more richness of BEing.

Those parts decided to separate, in mind, from the greater Void. We are those parts, figments if you will, that decided to take on various forms to experience, express, and expand the richness of *All That Is*.

We lost our way. After eons of forms and experiences, after eons of words and deeds, we forgot the nature of our True Self. There is only One, and right now in bodily form, we are a part of One. But that One is a part of something much, much greater, *All That Is*.

As near as I can determine, we placed layer upon layer to mask our True Self. It started long before Atlantis or Lemuria. Those were just epic turning points in our illusory history; times when we decided to take on increasingly denser form. Those days are long gone. In Truth, they never existed for this is a game of mind, the small mind in each figment.

We agreed to experience this realm of consciousness but lost sight of our God-given abilities. In the course of experiencing the dream, we continued to spiral into denser and denser realms, leaving our True Self behind.

As part of this experiment, we belong to a vast entity, Soul. Many call this the Oversoul. It consists of unique and vastly different souls, all playing the game of life on earth. Throughout time, each soul takes on new personalities, new experiences, new missions to experience, expand, and express the richness of *All That Is*.

As souls, we agree to forget our true nature before we take on a new form. Our form and the environment we choose offer us the perfect place to experience, expand, and express. This is just one part of our journey. And now, it is ending. I don't mean that in a negative way but only as a change, as in the change of earth seasons.

These are monumental times as we awaken to recognize our full potential. We are finally beginning to remember who we really are. The process of awakening is different for everyone but it is still a process. On earth, and perhaps other realms, we believe our soul needs to grow. And sometimes that soul has very different ideas on what experiences need to occur while the body is on earth. For some, listening to Angels, Spirits, and other guides seems necessary. And yet, we possess the best source of information within us. Many people refer to this source as the Higher or True Self.

A great disservice to humanity occurred when we invented words. Words are not important. And yet, at one point in our evolution, words became a way to communicate for the density of form became too much. Words are layers of fake reality but now we can use them to awaken.

LightworkersLog.com

The time to realize this is an illusion of our own making is here. Words, coupled with our sixth sense, lead the way out of the illusion. We are unique souls, parts of spirit now manifested in human form to experience life on earth. Our true nature is Love, pure unadulterated, unconditional Love. Many of us chose to lead or be an example for others to follow.

Yes, we are indeed Gods of Creation and I, as many others, chose before birth to wake up parts of me that are still asleep in the dream. Spirit blessed me during this earth experience to perceive many, vastly different, states of awareness. The bottom line is to learn unconditional love, unconditional love for everyone without a single thought of separation. Experience taught me that the unique Essence is within and we have only to listen to that one very subtle Voice. It is the Voice of inclusion and unconditional Love.

It is time to remember who we are and return to *All That Is*. My soul agreed to spread the word by discussing the many experiences that affected this physical body. If one is open-minded to believe beyond a rigid set of beliefs, one will clearly see, after learning of my experiences, that there is so much more to life than anyone could ever comprehend.

Humanity is one of an infinite number of entities and things that makes the whole of God. We are beautiful Light Beings, pure energy in material form, having a physical experience and it is now time to awaken the God within. The light of remembrance will glimmer brightly by the time you finish reading *Book of One :-)*.

Our thoughts and words make our physical reality and now that physical reality is manifesting quicker than ever before. It's vitally important that humans remain positive in thought for what we concentrate on manifests to become our reality.

It is my understanding that some souls chose to stay a bit longer in the dream of forgetfulness. But it's important to note *All That Is* has never, and will never, be disrupted.

LightworkersLog.com

One can see *All That Is* as a vast collage of everything that exists. One may take a photo of the collage and make a puzzle but it does not change the collage. One may separate the photo into unique puzzle parts but that has no affect on the collage either. One may even disconnect the parts of the puzzle and separate them to the four corners of the earth, and beyond, but it still has no affect on the original collage. Eventually, the puzzle parts will come together and disintegrate having never been 'real' at all. The photo will be no more, but the collage remains perfect, whole, and unaffected.

Humanity is part of the dream puzzle associated with the photo of the collage. Yet, there is nothing to separate us from *All That Is* but human thought.

My books help those lost in the maze to raise their energy sequentially. One of many surprising moments comes while drafting the fourth book. The light bulb in my head glows brightly as words fill my brain.

"This is not the book you are to write at this time. It is time to begin the *Book of One*."

Instantaneously, I know the book will hold many messages received over the past four years.

This is the *Book of One :-)*. It helps us to tap into the True Self.

Book of One :-)
Begins in Earnest

Tiredness overwhelms me after working too late on March 8, 2011 so I retire, without a shower, shortly after midnight. Falling asleep quickly, after a scant washing of key body parts, no longer concerns me. Waking up at three, four, or five o'clock in the morning, to read or work for hours, no longer concerns me. Erratic sleeping and waking hours no longer concern me because thankfully, I am physically alone. And unless I mention these hours, no one will ever know. What a well-deserved luxury this life, this body, lives.

A tall cup of enriched orange juice with a magnesium tablet sustains me upon waking before five o'clock in the morning. Jane Roberts entertains me with *The Seth Material* for the next hour until I sleep again. My reliable toy communication device remains silent but the messages continue upon waking.

"It is the hope of Consciousness to be one in the Light. It is the hope of Consciousness to never return to separation. This hope is held by tiny pieces that do not realize they are not really separate at all. These tiny pieces of Consciousness began their journey so many eons ago. But they have forgotten who, what, they truly are, parts of the great Whole, unable, in a dreamlike state, to return to Wholeness. These tiny parts of Consciousness return seemingly, one by one, to join the Whole again. And yet, it is a Whole that has never been segmented and never shall be unwhole.

"The truth of the matter is we make this world with our thoughts. We make everything with our thoughts for we are just a mind seeming to be in a body. There is no space.

There is no time. There is nothing but the emptiness, and the fullness, of Consciousness. There are tiny, white beings of Light all around you. Open your mind to see those tiny, white beings of Light and know they can be molded into a better reality. It is a reality already played out on other realms. It is a reality that has already ended in other realms. The truth of the matter is; Consciousness exists. Consciousness exists in what you would call everywhere, in everything, and yet, Consciousness is *All There Is.*"

My brain responds to a question asking if I'm ready to move on. The familiar energy field circulates around me as I readily agree and ask for more Light. A bit of ego fights for control, demanding a bathroom break, while my body happily absorbs more Light.

"Trust in the process," I hear, several minutes later upon sitting in the bathroom. "Don't be so concerned with writing the book you are now for you will be writing the *Book of One :-)*. It will be done by July 2012 but do not concern yourself with the timeline."

Confirmation comes once again, in an unexpected way, during a reading at The Modern Day Mystery School in Fort Lauderdale, Florida on November 4, 2011. Fourteen people take turns reading of the Seventh Ray: The Violet Flame of Transmutation from *Seven Sacred Flames*. School Founders remind us to pay particular attention to the part we read. People read until the text no longer resonates with them. The person to their left then continues reading.

The section I read verifies that people no longer care how I got to where I am now. It's the message of One that is important. For the past several months, I transcribed almost all my tapes to extract received messages. And now, I know that the two books, in draft form, are no longer important. Of course, there's always the chance they may be refined and published after *Book of One :-)*. But I seriously doubt it.

Upon returning home another message notes I am not to concern myself with anything, just to BE. Grace-filled times cushioned between prayer, meditation and spiritual study come to mind. Joy fills me upon remembering what it's like to merely BE. To be led, into previously unrecalled states of awareness, like the time Spirit guided me to the back yard of the house on 47th Drive to gaze at four, green hornets in wonder.

My nose, a mere inch away from the branch of flowers holding the hornets, does not know what the creatures are as a state of Oneness saturates the atmosphere. There's no memory to mar the experience with fear for I have no idea what the green creatures are. Much later, after this time of bliss, comes a knowing of what my eyes lovingly held on that sunny, summer day.

"That's the way to BE," I hear. "Just to BE, just to live in the wonder of BEing and trust in the process."

My brain knows *Book of One :-)*, will consist of channeled messages. How I got to this point makes no difference now. Perhaps the Preface will explain why I now concentrate on this book and maybe it will explain how I got to this state of channeling. But all that is history and there is no history. There is only BEing. History no longer matters. There is no longer a need to prove who I was for that person is gone, never to return. For that, I am evermore grateful.

Today is another gateway day. I catch myself visioning three beautiful homes intact with spiritual partner while taking in more Light. I'm now asking for, and receiving, allowing, more Light to fill body cells in every waking and sleeping moment. Yes, life is good!

:-)

The *Book of One :-)* is different from other books for it contains messages from the One of Love, Light, and Truth, the only one that exists in my small mind, for all else is illusion.

"The life we live here is a potpourri of dreaded and lovely moments in a time/space continuum, which never really exists. Everything is made with the power of thought and that power is the Power of God, the one everlasting Truth. There is no need to seek outside the Self for the Self is a part of God, a fragment lost in a sea of consciousness that is finally finding its way back to the Wholeness of I AM.

"The *Book of One* is a personal effort to clear the past of ill thought, which permeated earth eons ago. It is a blessing of Love and Light, unduly (disproportionately) a part of the Whole of One. The day of reckoning that many believe will occur is not coming but in its place, a glorious state of awareness continues to grow in the minions that occupy earth.

"Be still and know that you are the Light of God in which I am well pleased. Know that the spirit spark within you holds the unique Light of God in each, wholly unmarred by falsities of the illusionary past. It is all you really need to know.

"Follow the one of Light to find your way. There are many before you to choose from and each will reckon forth the Light of One in its entirety. Play no games upon the presence of One for you live within it, your very being. The spirit spark within you glows brightly with each thought of Wholeness. Seek nothing but the spark within."

:-)

The message of One flows through my earthly essence while listening to a CD play erratically. The earth and people upon her are going though radical changes now. I am not to speak of them but to hold the Light so all can see how easy it is to maintain composure in the face of difficulty. This is what I have been guided and trained to do over the past four years. It is an action of love for the One of *All That Is*.

LightworkersLog.com

Feeling the energy course though my hands as I peck away at the keyboard fills me with a calm assurance that what I type is indeed a necessary part for the book. Honesty, I do still have doubts and sometimes ignore the messages that begin to come though. Over the years, my skill of honing and receiving messages has improved as I pay more attention to the subtle nuances of Spirit. And yet, as most humans, ego does not wish to be bothered at certain times.

"Enough," I hear, as the music stops before the CD plays through.

"The light of One is already victorious but the masses will not believe this truth for a bit of time to come. Nevertheless, we the Lightworkers must continue to hold the Light of Truth. It is our duly appointed task and one that is ever wanted by those that seek to come here to earth."

I must hold the Light within and shine it forth for all to reap the pleasure of one Truth, that we are One, never having parted. The sanity we seek is already ours. It is just a matter of living it in the Light of One.

"Take care in the days ahead," I hear now. "For the days of mass hysteria come quickly. Do not be dissuaded by the masses that know not yet of their true essence. You, as others, will continue to guide the way to Truth bearing the Light in all circumstances. Hear nothing outside the realm of One, for there will be many that speak not from within. Go forth knowing all is Almighty One and nothing can interfere with the Light you, and others, carry.

"No truth abides outside the One but be glorious in the Light within. That is the Light of One. You are ever presently aware of the goings on of mass consciousness but must not feed the thoughts of those that seek less than perfection. Know that the One within is inherently perfect in all ways. It is your Source, your Truth, your Life.

"I am aware of your struggle within to play this game of limited life and yet we both know your choice, the choice,

LightworkersLog.com

is already made. The Light Bearers will achieve their rightful accomplishment regardless of naysayers. The Truth exists within where it cannot be manipulated or carelessly harmed by outside forces. The spark of One lies inside, unharmed and unafraid, regardless of appearances in the physical body. That is a Truth to regard and spread among the masses. Be not afraid of yourself for you are an eternal being with powers way beyond the scope of your limited form."

:-)

"One reaps the wholeness of Truth when one bears the Light. This wholeness is everlasting in its glory and power to shed the ways of yore. Olden days fade quickly as the New Earth takes shape before your very eyes. These are the same eyes that shaped the earth so many eons ago. It is time to change the tide of never ending woe and transform it to a tsunami, of inner peace and beauty that never ceases. The role of all Lightworkers is to bring forth that within you that bears the Light of God. This truth is known to few but many will hearken to the call soon as the gross changes take place on Mother Earth.

"Hear nothing of false reports of discord for they are meant to dissuade one from the Inner Light within. There is and shall never be a separation. There is nothing outside the face or avenue of One but only a wholeness of purity and perfection. Know this and be secure in the wholeness of Self for truly all that matters is the security of BEing.

"The time to reap old sown seeds gathers closer as we near the final point of change for Mother Earth. It will be a massive change from what you know today. Do not let fear guide your way but stay steadfast in the truth of One, leaving all thought of separation behind.

"The time has come to return to the Godhead in all aspects. It has been too long; hence, the Mind of One beckons the call to further evolution of earth and all its inhabitants. Turn back the small clocks of the mind of the little self, for those clocks, as all else, are illusion, and cannot ever be paraded with Truth.

"Feel the Oneness of all Life within, as you move though the chaos that surrounds you, for now the only way to Truth is through turmoil. This effect will not last long, in earthly senses, but will continue unabated for many days to come. The change Mother Earth seeks is one of eliminating the impurities within from eons of disuse and abuse. Let not these changes continue to affect the illusion of your making.

"Feel, and sense, the illusionary nature of your surroundings and know that when you sleep, when in tune with the One, you are closer to the truth of your Self. It is the truth of One, everlasting and wholly perfect, powerful beyond all thought."

`~`~ Glimmers of Light `~`~

When Daniel, the spirit of my last-born son, began to speak to me after his transition there was no clue that the messages would change in time. His essence eventually led me to what we referred to as "Higher Beings." Messages of One began as single sentences that grew longer over time. Sometimes they seemed to come from Jesus as I studied *A Course In Miracles*. Sometimes, I did not understand messages until years later.

Perhaps words such as these enter your thoughts as well. If so, here's hoping this book will help you to understand that you are one of many called forth to spread the word of One. Contemplating one message each day may be rewarding.

`~`~`~`~

"Go to the path of God directly. Take care of all your brothers and sisters and you shall be rewarded."

`~`~`~`~

"I will show the way to those good of heart."

`~`~`~`~

"Yea, though I die, yet shall I live."

`~`~`~`~

"Love is all there is in this perfect world of love, peace, and harmony."

`~`~`~`~

"Awake and be free."

Lightworkers Log.com

"We supply the Word by sharing our skills."

"Prepare the way further."

"Have faith, keep your faith. God's Will is done by you."

"As you light the way for others, I shall light the way for you."

"You shall learn the ways of the Lord. The Truth shall reveal its Self to you."

"The path is true and I shall guide you all the way."

"Blessings be upon you now."

"All things in time, sayeth the Lord."

"God is the Creator of all living things."

"Love is all there is."

"Victory is the mainstay of fear."

"We are in a constant state of influx."

"There is nothing between the illusion and the soul."

"Then within a day, within the last few minutes, we shall be called Home."

"Our relocation is a process."

"You give what you got and you get more."

"You can change your perceptions of earth very beyond what you have here."

"The story is ongiving love."

"You're observing grace from a beautiful point of earth."

"There is unity even without knowledge. One day we will be united as One again."

"You must go slow. You must train your mind to accept the Truth. You have all you need for a joyous and spontaneous life."

"The form doesn't matter. We are all the same."

LightworkersLog.com

"You will learn the truth."

"A path will show the way."

"To perceive your abundance as loss is not good."

"Forget your humanness. Be one with *All*."

"Holy Moses taught all his brethren, one by one, to be one with God. And the Truth shall set you free."

"The truth about you, has been, and always will be."

"We will never leave you. We are One."

"The lights of communication are the key, the key to *All*."

"In your mind, God continues to hold you in present."

"Don't ever dull the senses that are filled with love and cheer."

"The truth be told, all sins are great."

"Just touch, touch, touch to your body to heal."

"We in common are guided toward the light."

"*All* is the all to search for on this earth."

"All things in time."

"We have all come from the same place."

"We are not human beings. We are other entities."

"We are often fooled by appearances."

"You are the Light."

"It is all God. God is *All*."

"Lift up thine eyes unto the Lord and see the greatness therein."

"We are all saints."

"The human body is a vessel for the Lord."

"Pray as the presence of the living God. Healing is a movement of consciousness within the one doing the work, recognizing we are all one. One I AM that I AM."

"Pay attention to symbols."

"Be still and know that I am God."

"The gift of life is precious."

"Do not look outside yourself."

"Remember, you are the Way."

"The signs are forthcoming."

"And everybody is part of someone else."

"You are a child of God. You have been given mercy."

"Stay the course. The path is true."

"Choose carefully from the tree of life."

"Bask in the light of the Lord."

LightworkersLog.com

"Your soul will always be in God."

"It is a gift unmatched by any other to awaken one's soul to the essence of their being."

"The highest God is the innermost God, the one that must be received."

"There is beauty everywhere. You have only to take it all in."

"The sense of separation is no more."

"God is neither man, woman, or child but the God-head, One, *All*."

"This is where we want to be, in the garden where there is no cold, no warm. There is only the warm love of God, enveloping, enveloping, enveloping."

"You can not escape your destiny. You must show others the glory of their dreams. Their light shines as bright as yours."

"We are here to glorify the presence of God."

"You are the Light of God with whom I am well pleased. Always speak the truth for you speak the words of God."

LightworkersLog.com

"This is the best time that you can be someone to give to all."

"God exists in only one state of unconditional love, truth, perfection. Our supposed separation will never be recognized by the One."

"Meet the new day refreshed in the glory of God."

"As we let our light shine out into the Godhead, the Universe sends it's combined Light into us."

"The sunshine of God is within you. Let it pour out to all things."

"The abundance of God is all around you. To feed the abundance of God you must feed everyone around you with love, with joy."

"Each one, at each time, blossoms and grows."

"God's timing is crucial. You must pay attention to the details of the timing."

"Remember the One. What you do to yourself, you do to another. What you do to another, you do to yourself."

LightworkersLog.com

"The Will of God is One."

"Go forth with a blessing upon your heart for you are free."

"Surround yourself in joy, abundance and Truth."

"Use your free will wisely."

"Go with God for God is with you."

"All is new. Begin your day refreshed."

"You are well loved."

"All things pass sayeth the Lord."

"One needs to always think of this life in better terms of living."

"Feel the healing energy of the Lord your Savior. It gives me great joy to give this to you."

"All is well. All is according to plan."

"There is something to be said for waiting. Divine Order will prevail."

"The eyes of the Lord are upon you. Be secure in the Truth."

"The others are waiting on the Otherside. We need only to acknowledge them and they will help us get Home."

"Continue to act out of Love. Have Faith in God. Have Faith in our Father. Remember you are a spirit and not a human."

"The Lord is with you. Never fear for thou art the holy one of the Lord thy God."

"You are a virtuous soul."

"We are One, *All*."

"Keep the Faith. Your Lord is watching."

"There's nothing to do. Things will come to you."

"Heal well my friend and go forth and spread the Word."

"God is ever with you. Do not be afraid."

LightworkersLog.com

"This earth's nothing in the grand scheme of things. What's important is getting all back to the One."

"God is in all things great and small."

"You are perfect, whole, and complete, a part of the One. There is no other way to be but completely whole and perfect."

"Seeing into space and calling to the Other makes thy dreams come true."

"Ye are one with the Living Spirit Almighty. Arise and be free."

"Go in peace my sister for you are free. Trust in the Lord with all thy heart."

"Forget about the human stuff. You are perfect, whole, and complete."

"Steady be thy faith in the Lord thy God."

"Thy words are as powerful as the Lord thy God."

"Thou art with the Lord God Almighty. To thine own Self be True."

LightworkersLog.com

"Arise oh ye holy one and let nothing sway thee from the Truth."

"There are many clues so one must understand them inside out."

"Whether it be sinus (issues) or cutting the cord (from earthly matters) go to the Lord thy God for thy help."

"Arise and seek the Lord for he is not hard to find."

"A change in attitude to the positive must always be instilled."

"The time is ripe. The hour is near. Your liberty is at hand. Feast not upon things not of thy Lord. It is God's Will you finish your work. It will be done."

"This is a dream world. You can do anything you want as long as you don't hurt other people."

"Carry on in the spirit and truth of God."

"Thy love abounds from within, go forth knowing ye are free."

LightworkersLog.com

"To those who wait come the riches of the world. The work is done and praise abounds."

"I am here and will never leave you."

"Be still and know that I am the Savior of all, the keeper of the Mind, and I am with you always."

"You are the Living Spirit Almighty. Arise and shine in the spirit of the Lord."

"Be still and know that I AM the Light of God and shall be with you always."

"There is no pain. There is only Truth in the Lord Jesus."

"Go forth in awe and wonder of the world that lies before you, for ye are One."

"Go ye forth strident in the purpose of spreading the word of the Lord."

"Let the healing energy of the Lord pour through you and be one with *It*."

"Perfection is in the eye of the beholder. See only perfection and you will be it."

"One is a call to BEing. One is united effort."

"You're a spirit in human form. Remember, you're a spirit in human form."

"There is still time in securing the future of the humans on earth. Remember daily to hear the words of the Lord. Thy God is always with thee."

"We are all one with God."

"The circle of life flows within me forever now."

"I am one with the universe."

"BEing is centeredness."

"The truth will be told through you and as you tell the truth, so shall you heal."

"It is done as you believe. Be careful what you believe for it is done as you believe."

"Homosexuality is the gender of Reality. Homosexuality is chosen by truly enlightened souls, wishing to finish their karmic obligation to one another and to themselves, to the world in general."

~·~·~·~·~

"You must listen to the Voice inside you to sustain you."

~·~·~·~·~

"The past is no more. The future is no more. The time is Now, forevermore."

~·~·~·~·~

"There is no time. There is no space. It is only on earth that we believe this."

~·~·~·~·~

"Live a life unlimited."

~·~·~·~·~

"Listen to the heretics."

~·~·~·~·~

"Rise and spread the word of God."

~·~·~·~·~

"God's Will is done when our free will meets that of the greater good."

~·~·~·~·~

"To be one with the Most High is the only necessity."

~·~·~·~·~

"In the heart of it all is the Love and energy that we hold for one another."

~·~·~·~·~

LightworkersLog.com

"The truth is that we are One. The Oneness doesn't end just because you seem to lose the connection. Oneness is always there free to partake of."

"Fear is bad for you. It will eat your heart some."

"Stop listening to the world and pay attention to spirit."

"Just go with the flow. We will guide you. You are free of the constraints of this world."

"Life is not to be planned. Life is to be lived in the Now. Life becomes what you concentrate on so it's important not to concentrate on anything you don't want in your life."

"Just listen to your heart center, the thing you call your heart center."

"Listen well my friend for you are chosen to lead the masses."

"God's Will is done through you forevermore."

"Concentrate on defined areas of consciousness. BEing is Oneness. BEing is Centeredness, are examples."

"One is to be attracted by energy."

LightworkersLog.com

˚⸍˚⸍˚⸍˚⸍

"Create from the Creator."

˚⸍˚⸍˚⸍˚⸍

"As we speak yellow mind, we become yellow mind."

˚⸍˚⸍˚⸍˚⸍

"We are one in the likes of God."

˚⸍˚⸍˚⸍˚⸍

"Rise in the knowledge that God is with you my child. Be not afraid. Be joyful in the One. I am with you always."

˚⸍˚⸍˚⸍˚⸍

"This holy plan of commitment dwells in the heart of hearts forevermore. This holy plan of commitment is One."

˚⸍˚⸍˚⸍˚⸍

"Keep your guard up. The interference will lessen for you in time and you will need no guard. That's it. Rest easy in the knowledge of the One."

˚⸍˚⸍˚⸍˚⸍

"We are one with the Living Spirit Almighty. Go with that truth and know it."

˚⸍˚⸍˚⸍˚⸍

"Continue on your path for it is true. Things will come to you in the spirit of the Lord."

˚⸍˚⸍˚⸍˚⸍

"Every moment counts."

˚⸍˚⸍˚⸍˚⸍

"Please know everything is within my time."

"Go whitherest thy may for you are healed. All is well in your world, for you are a Light of God."

"Lead with faith my little one for you are the Light of the Lord."

"You are called upon to witness the power of the Lord."

"Begin the day renewed."

"Seek not outside yourself for the world is within."

"You shall need things to prepare you."

"Speak not of hate, of woe, duress. There is only love for God to bless."

"Know ye what you seek is inside."

"Seek not what is outside yourself for all is within."

"Begin the day refreshed in the name of the Lord."

"Rise in joy and praise of the Lord thy God, Yahweh."

"Everyday is a new beginning."

"Time, we know is an illusion and space as well. What we know as a reality is our Oneness."

"Just know that all things come to you easily now. Don't sweat the small stuff."

"As time goes on, and people realize all the good within them, bodies will heal much more quickly."

"Go to the path of higher thinking."

"The path of spiritual influence will take you Home."

"In certain lives we are faced with abuse, and in others we are surrounded with animals that help us to transcend that abuse through their use of unconditional love."

"Don't make things harder than they need to be. Just go with the flow."

"Don't worry. All is well. Believe in the power of the One."

"Let me forget the patterns of exclusion as I move forward in time to its end."

LightworkersLog.com

"The choice is yours to make. Using your free will you choose and change your environment."

"Connecting with our soul we learn the truth of our BEing. The Oversoul, the soul, it is all an illusion of our own making. One is all there is."

"Everything in your life has to match the vibration level that you are seeking."

"All things are relative to form. Each cell holds it's own clues to awareness. Each form holds its own constructs to meaning. The constructs of living are difficult to understand for the unbeliever. It's a call to rise, to rise out of limitation."

"For in the twinkling of an eye, ye shall come Home."

"You are filled with spiritual energy and Light."

"You see the wonders of *All* easily now and forevermore. You are free."

"The past is gone and it's time to move on."

"God's energy field is hovering above your head and you can tap into it at any time. You've done so before."

LightworkersLog.com

"You can make it worth your while. You can change it to good, beyond limits."

"Function as awareness of Self."

"The steepness of the ladder depends on your perception."

"The Light of God is within you. Go forth and spread the news."

"I transmute all negativity and bring it to the Light."

"We are One, living in a state of grace, through the power of God."

"*All That Is* is within you."

"Let go of the past. Live in the Now. That's the key."

"Nowadays there are many things to concentrate on. The One is the only concentration you need; the one of *All That Is*, the wholly One, within the soul."

"Look around at the beauty around you. That beauty is yours to admire, nurture and grow."

"The cataclysms of the earth will return mirroring Pompeii. They will stop as the people come together as One."

"Easter Sunday you will discover the secrets of life upon learning the despair."

"The last times of age are with you now."

"Be true to thine own Self."

"*All* is here. *All* is One. *All* is now.

"We are one unalterable loving Source."

"Of course, we will stay with you and increase. Never fear, all is well."

"God is ever with you. Do not be afraid. Go about your business in each and every way."

"You are one with the universe. The universe is one with you."

"Just continue to draw in the Light of God and know that all is well. Continue with your studies."

"Your ultimate responsibility is to nurture earth, and all upon it."

"Draw in the energy of One, for that, is what you are. Spread the Word."

"The One in which we live is all around you. Feel it and relish in the One."

"Love, and Light, and Truth of our Oneness, let it spread."

"These wounds are not real. They are a recording in the Matrix that must be changed. Change them, the thought."

"We need to believe this is a time where everyone can change the energy around the experiences they have had (as souls in every life). Everyone can change this energy and make things better for themselves. All they need do is envision what occurred and envision a different experience."

"Can you envision a world where everything is of your liking? That world is possible and it begins with you. By changing your world to the world you wish to live in, by being the one you wish to be, that world quickly morphs into Heaven on Earth."

"After Light initiation, I move directly to Source."

"The sight of One becomes the sight of many. Know this and be free."

"Love is everywhere. It is yours to keep, to claim. Expand your BEing and feel it caress you. Feel it flow into you. Feel the Love flow out from you reaching everything and everyone, now, and always."

"Religion is not the way to go. Your message is One, the Truth, the Light, the Whole."

"You can provide the impetus for many to move toward the Light."

"We are being led. We must cling to that belief."

"Remember, everything is magnetics. Just go with the magnetic force around you. Flow into it. Picture those tiny, white beings of Consciousness. Merge with the magnetics around you. Merge with the One and know that all is well."

"The mountain you seek to climb is only within. There is no struggle or strife. Today is a day of pure grace."

"In all you say, in all you do, these precious words I give to you. Be strong, have faith, your path is true. There is no one outside of you."

"Each have our own role in this world. And yet, we all have one thing in common. We are bringing in more Light to the world. We are leaders of One."

"Integrity is not a body."

"I go before thee to guide the way. Do not be afraid."

"His presence is everywhere and everything."

"We have forgotten how to create but now we remember and it is time to create all those things that we wish."

"One Light, one Love, one Truth, ever expanding in Consciousness."

"Like energy attracts like energy. There are no exceptions. Be careful what you think."

"The birth of a new home is necessary. This new home supersedes all limitations of earth."

"All is well. Do not fear in the days ahead for the days of woe are numbered."

LightworkersLog.com

"All is well. Divine Order, Divine Timing prevails. Fear not."

"There are no discarnate energies of the soul. It is only the mind that is purified and cleansed. When we think that we are clearing discarnate energies from the soul, it's only the mind because there is no soul. It is only the mind which needs to be healed of discarnate energies."

"Each day changes and brings us newer realities."

"One man, many lives, all illusion."

"The way of the One is ever-present. Centeredness abides below."

"New and exciting business awaits those that wish to pass to the other side."

"Life is not to be lived. It is to be experienced."

"The powers of manifestation lie within you. Use them wisely."

"Permit yourself the freedom to ride the wave of Consciousness."

"All is well my friend as we reconnect to re-member."

"The sheeple will lead the people out of the mass consciousness of duality."

"Listen to me now for the ways of Truth are upon you and you know that to be true. Give up the old reality of this disdainful world. Let go of the old energies and take on the new ones in joy, in truth, and in the love that you came here to spread."

"We are the resurrection race."

"Light extends in every measure throughout the field of One."

"Soul chose to not be trapped in a body. Soul chose to continue into Light."

"Sometimes the road is treacherous but do not worry. The Almighty Lord is with you now, paving the way to glory. Knowing all things on your earth are illusion will make the path easier to bear. *All That Is*, and ever will be, lives in the moment of NOW. Use it wisely."

"As you go forward toward the new Babylon, know that all things exist in time. The time of your world is nonexistent on other planes for there is no time yet desired to be."

LightworkersLog.com

"Rise and be fruitful in the ways of the Lord. The days of the Golden Age are upon you."

"Your Self of One speaks for its self whenever you seek the answers to mundane questions of life."

"Moving is a state of mind for those ready to let the 3-D reality go. You know it is all in the mind yet you persist in knowing the Truth of your reality is not within yourself. Know this Truth as unerring."

"I love you. I am physically in love with that presence that is you. And yet, there is no physical. There is no you. There is only One and you are that One, so loved, part of the Creator, part of the One. Goodnight."

^ Flashes of True BEing *^*

"The safest land in the U.S. offers a safe haven to ensure the enlightened have a place wherein they may perform their greatest work. This task ensures the greater good of all humanity. Safe land and a safe and secure fortress await the chosen people right before the end of the days."

* * * *

"The 'call to arms' is real, in this world, for the angels of God must fight the dark forces. Although you may not believe in them, many others do. Hence, the need to overcome the fear and the distraught of those dark forces exist. The teacher of God shall help them overcome those dark forces."

* * * *

"Feel the peace of God within you. As you seek so shall you heal. As you seek, so shall the glory of God continue to grow within you. There's a time and a purpose for everything. As you work, so shall you heal."

* * * *

"The cosmic rays of energy fill the skies with their glory. The cosmic rays of Light and Love are yours to behold in all goodness. And peace and hope abound on this great earth, that is not knowing, or yet to know, that it is One."

* * * *

"I am here to show others that there is another way. One need not believe in limitation, whether of a financial sort, or of body or mind. Thoughts are things and we can train our thoughts. It may take some time. We may be tested. But eventually, we can come to the One, to the one Principle, to the one knowledge that we are perfect.

"We are perfect spirits. And although we are in body-mind form, that perfection exists in body-mind form as well. We need only to train our mind to recognize it is so. Just because we are in a body does not mean that we are imperfect. We must train our bodies. We must train our minds. And although it may take a weaning of drugs, and a weaning of thoughts, we will eventually get to that point where we recognize that we are perfection. Our body renews daily. A simple reminder throughout the day will help."

* * * *

"All are One. There is no other. There is only the One. There is only the one perfect Light. And that Light is always in you and it is good. It views all things from the other side. It is always available. It is always coming. It is always there. The help from the other side is unerring.

"You have lost your constitutional right to be free but this is just a play world. It is the world of your choosing. What you think affects the mold. It's the knowing that you are part of something bigger than yourself that is your saving grace. Hear me when I speak. It is well. All is good. Do not be fearful. You are being guided from on high even when you have no idea and when you don't think it. Even when you don't feel it, you are being guided from on high. You are never alone. You need not fear. All is One and yet One is *All*.

"Within each one, within each core is the core of the God, the Savior, the One, unerringly perfect within you and all things, self-fulfilling, guiding, and futuristic. All is God. There is no drama, only what you make in the mind and the mind is limited. Beware of the mind. Beware of the thoughts of the mind. You are all One. God is *All*. You are all One.

"Know you are guided from on high. Know you are not alone. Know we are One. That's all. We are One."

* * * *

Lightworkers Log.com

"There are no limitations now. We are all free, a part of God's massive universe. Within the universe we are all part of God, all seeing, all knowing, where all possibilities exist. There is no limitation. It is only in our mind, in our physical human hearts; in our minds, that we believe there is limitation. There is no limitation on earth. There is no limitation at all; stop thinking of limitation."

* * * *

"There is only One. You know that to be the Truth. Everything that you need is inside you and will come forth when you need it. Spread the word. Christ has awakened within us. It is time for the great awakening."

* * * *

"Best as you can you must clear the way for the others. The others know nothing of what is to come. You must clear the way for them. You must help to instill within them, in their heart core, in their heart center, the one Living Spirit Almighty that is already there. You will know when and who to do this with. We will continue to guide you. Do not be afraid. Do not fear for God is with you always. Do not be afraid. Do not fear. We are the One. We are the one Living Spirit Almighty within you. We shall speak at other times."

* * * *

"Rest, your fortune is not of this world but you shall live well here. There is much work to be done and you shall begin it anew, refreshed in the Lord thy God, refreshed in the Source of the One."

* * * *

"The time is ripe for the people have been told. The ways of God are shown to the people that follow the words of the Lord, the wayshowers. The wayshowers shall overcome all fear.

"You must go now to another place (in your mind) where there is Light and Love, where there is more hope for the future, for above. You must go to this place without fail, without tarry. It is your place to BE, to act as One, as God. What with all things shall come to you. Know this to be thy truth that all things come to you, wholly, astutely, honestly and kindly. Knowing this to be true, seek the way of the wayshowers. The wayshowers shall show the way and all will be well.

"We are with you now. Do not be afraid. The Lightbeings will guide you. We all have our own specialty and we are shown in that way to show the others. So know that your way is true for your specialty is to show the way to the Light, to the One, back to the Whole, back to the God of your BEing. Know this and seek nothing else. This is the wisdom of the ages. This is the truth of the Lord.

"Now is waiting, waiting to show the way. Don't be afraid. Fear only holds you back.

"LIVE, know thyself, and LOVE.

"A new day is dawning to save humanity with this necessary piece. We strongly advise staying clear of outside interference to the Light.

"Document well how the process unfolds for those that follow will need to know how it is done. The road is weary and long for they tarnish the truth of lies. The Truth shall shine forth and be known to all. Quickly, surely, soon the Truth will be known and you as a wayshower will show them the way. That is all I have to say at this time. Be it known that you are the one to follow. Be it known that you are the Light. Be it known, all are One, one Supreme Almighty Force of the universe, the only living matter, the only one that is holy.

"You know what the message is: Be true to thyself for you are the Lord thy God and there is none other than you.

"You will break through the gate of your words and others will follow. You will break through this gate knowing that all is One. You will break through this gate knowing there is none other for you are *All* and *All* is One. Come with me now to the golden gates of thy Lord, thy God, the one and only. Truth be told through you. Listen well, and it shall be known that all who come, come through the grace of God. It is so. I have spoken now and forevermore. One Truth, one BEing, one Light, One.

"Now the mark of the Lord is upon you. Know this to be true. You shall see it in all you seek and all you don't. The mark of the Lord is upon you. The time has come to speak the Truth, the Truth of the Lord. Go now and be safe in the Truth of the Lord. Pay no mind to this world for this world is naught. This world is naught."

* * * *

"You are a wayshower. You must show the way to the others. The Light shines within you, out over the land, the land of Truth, the land of Light, the land of Reality. You are a wayshower. The land of Truth is within, within all, something that is sorely needed to know. Spread the word. The Word of God is within all. Listen and hear. The way of the Lord is nigh. The Light is everlasting. You are the Light. The true light of your being is Light, safe in the bosom of the Lord.

"I know things are not as easy as they seem, and yet, you must continue on the journey, the journey of Light. You must continue on the path approving no one, and yet, approving all. You must remember to be one with the Light. There is none other. There is only the Light. The Light is the Truth, the truth of your BEing and you know that to be true. Stay safe in the bosom of the Lord. Ignore the reports around you. There is none other; there is only the Light. Stay safe in the bosom of the Light. That is all I came to tell you. Stay safe in the bosom of the Light. Ignore the reports around you.

"And so it begins my friend. The time is near, time for all humanity to change back into the One. Sleepiness continues for quite a while but the time is nigh for change. The change becomes increasingly more with each passing day. Prepare for the change within and without. The change will be strong keeping you on your toes evermore. Just know that all is well in this land of what seems to be woe.

"Draw in the energy of One for that is what you are."

* * * *

"Don't take anything seriously for this world is an illusion. The inherent truth of your BEing is not in this illusion. Pave the way for those who come quickly now. We now will forego The Fall."

* * * *

"They know what they are doing. Let them be. They know the time is now. The time is now for the end, the end of the illusion, the end of the dream. They (new souls) come quickly now in hordes. They know what they are doing. Leave them alone. Let them be. They are meeting their call to wake the others. Count on the truth of your call to help the others."

* * * *

"The more we do it the more we remember. But you must first remember that it can occur. The more we do it, the easier it is to tap into that Consciousness of which we all are. Like anything else, it is a learned behavior. But this learned behavior sets us free."

* * * *

"You are, oh, so loved and being carefully watched. Your purging process is almost complete and soon the trials of this world will be totally behind you. You will be okay."

* * * *

"The BEing known as *Truth* is One. There can be no other.

LightworkersLog.com

Stand clear of the chaos around you, turn to God. The God within will comfort and restore. There is none other. The truth has no value in this world, for it is unknown to the past, and the future."

* * * *

"We are spirits in human form. We take on these bodies and use them as tools so that we may experience more. So that we may experience what it's like to be in a body. There are so many things to experience from being in a body and this is the only way we can experience them.

"But yet, in choosing the body, we've come to the point where we forget who we really are, spirits in human form, playing a game, the game of human life. We are unlimited. We've just forgotten."

* * * *

"The truth is you have to maintain an upbeat attitude with your thoughts. All thoughts are vibrations. All thoughts go out into space, the space that you are in and beyond. It's important to maintain positive thoughts. And go with those thoughts that you wish to come back to you, for those are the nurturing thoughts.

"The thoughts from day to day life are distracting and can be let go as soon as they enter the mind. You need not hang onto these thoughts. You need not hang onto the thoughts of others day-to-day lives either. The nurturing thoughts are those that are of Love. The nurturing thoughts are those that are of Peace. The nurturing thoughts are those that are of Light. Those are the thoughts to maintain in the head. Those are the thoughts to send out in those vibrational waves that go beyond your space and out into the space of others.

"This is the truth for everyday. You have asked for this truth and it has always been yours. It is done as you believe. Remember, it is done as you believe."

* * * *

"While we make our thoughts with our world there's a collective consciousness out there that sometimes intrudes on those thoughts, if we are not guarding our mind accurately. When we understand how thoughts, in the collective consciousness, affect us, it is another thing to guard against. Those of you who wish to avoid the idea of hell, avoid the idea of separation. It is the idea of separation that leads to the idea of hell. You must know this in your body, in your mind, in your soul. Instill this truth for there is no separation. There is only Love and God, and God is Love.

"Believing in the Oneness of us all takes us to a whole new level. Believing in the Oneness of us all sets us free from the mass consciousness that intrudes upon our thoughts. This mass consciousness disappears as we concentrate on the One of *All That Is*. We are a part of this One.

"You are alone in your universe of thinking. We are all each individual universes. We have the free will to do as we please. When we use that free will to merge into the Oneness, we are free from outside interferences. The Mind is a powerful thing to waste. The Mind of One overpowers the mind of separation. These thoughts are consistent with your beliefs for God is One, God is *All*, God is Love.

"Clear your mind to the truth of your BEing. You are one great almighty soul on an earth ride, a ride of discovery and wonder, a ride of joy and peace."

* * * *

"This is where you've always kept it, in your heart core. There's no side-stepping this truth. The Truth of the One lives though you. The truth of the *Almighty BEing* is One. The Truth of the One lives through us all. In allowing *It* to live, we live as One unerring truth on a sea of knowledge.

"*It* gives you knowing relief to heal the wounds of the world. Those wounds, just as this earth, are an illusion and shall soon disappear. This world, this earth, will not support those wounds any longer. Those wounds signify a separation from the One, which is not. There is no separation from the One. The game is over for you now. You know the Truth. You must continue on your path of wholeness. You must continue on your path of peace for you will make great changes in this world.

"You are not the only one making these changes. The collective consciousness is coming together. The call has been heard and many have awakened to the Consciousness of the One. Many are reporting such as you. It is with those that are reporting that you shall align yourself more closely with in this illusion. It is with those that speak the truth that you shall find your community. It is with those writers, those authors that speak of the One, those publishers, those artists that speak of the One. These are your 'peoples' as you call them.

"There's only One. It is only on this earth that separation appears to exist. Listen closely my child for these words are true. Make and bring yourself along this world with your thoughts. Guard your thoughts carefully and wholly and you shall find the peace within you. And it is in this peace that you shall dwell. It is in this peace that you shall find a safe haven throughout this storm. This is the peace of God that lies within. This haven shall be no more for those who continue to seek separation. Relish in the safety of this haven for those that seek it are free. And so it is."

* * * *

"We are brothers and sisters of soul in the Light, ever strengthening the Matrix in which we live. And that Matrix grows as we grow. And that Matrix strengthens as we strengthen. And that Matrix is never-ending. We are part of that fine Matrix, that substance of life that sustains us, and we feed that Matrix with our thoughts. Just as in the book you read (*The Divine Matrix* by Gregg Bradden), thoughts, beliefs, make the physical manifestations in your life.

"Carefully chosen thoughts, those are the thoughts to be nurtured. Those are the thoughts that will make the best life. You must tell your brothers and sisters this. You must let them know that these thoughts go into that ever-flowing Matrix and become their life, eventually, whether in this so-called life or the next. There is only one Matrix, and the Beings that form it, and the Beings that hold it together are One. Go forth and spread the word of the Matrix. You have been heard. What you seek is already found."

* * * *

"Now is the time to speak your truth. Now is the time to be heard. You join the others in speaking the words of God. You join the others in speaking the truth. And when it appears that the wrath of God has come, remember, there is no wrath of God. It is only the wrath of the mind, the mind in which you dwell, the mind in which you feed your thoughts.

"Those thoughts that are negative, those thoughts that keep you in the mind, don't pay attention to those thoughts. Those thoughts are not real. Those thoughts are needlessly cumbersome. Those thoughts are not of the One Mind. Free yourselves and your brothers. Free yourselves and your sisters for you are all One. There is no separation. You are all One and soon that shall become increasingly clear. You all know it within you."

* * * *

"Let the love spread out from your heart's core to everyone and everything. Don't ever forget that. You alone are responsible for your own well-being. There is no one above or below you. You alone make up this place you call home. Remember this as we move further into the Land of Oz, the land of illusion."

* * * *

"Yes, I believe there is a good we get lost in. This good fills our thoughts with woe, with distain for the future and the past. This good is nothing but our thoughts. We can edit this memory easily in dreams. Go into your dreams. Seek out those memories, those memories of disdain and distrust. Seek them out and change them. Change those memories to joyous Oneness with all. Change those memories to wealth, to love, to health. Change those memories and see the world change around you in your waking moments. It is easily done."

* * * *

"Everything will change because of these storms. You must be ready. You must be ready to lead and serve, for it is foretold, your destiny is set and you are ready to follow. The ways of the Lord are with you now. Be not afraid. As you lead, so shall you follow those that are on the path before you. The path is steady and sure and you shall follow them with sure footage. There is no other way for the path you follow is sure."

* * * *

"The time is ripe for destruction of the planet that you know is yours. But it will not happen. Things are changing rapidly, quickly, more quickly than you can imagine. Hang tight as the New Earth begins to emerge. Hang tight as this New Earth blossoms in every possible way. Hang tight as old thoughts are replaced with new. It's happening now."

* * * *

"Trust in the Lord thy God, for the Lord thy God is the Way, the only Way, the only Truth, the only One. Trust in the Lord. The Lord thy God is the Way, the only Way, the Truth, the Light. Trust in the Lord. There's nothing to be saved from. Trust in the Lord, thy God, the Light.

"Know ye that ye are One, one everlasting Principle of Life. The maze before you is not real. The illusion exists

LightworkersLog.com

for only a short time. Let it fade into the nothingness in which it came. Know ye, we are One and the Truth of the Lord speaks through each.

"Know ye, all is an illusion but the Light is everlasting. Know this and be safe in the Lord, in the god of your heart, the one Whole.

"There are a few things that you must do to secure the area, to secure yourself for the rough days ahead. These things in time will come to you. The time is nigh for soon the world will change never to return to the old ways.

"Hear ye and speak thy truths. The time is nigh.

"Listen and seek not outside yourself. The world is behind you now, the world that never was and never shall be.

"Enjoy the energies. Let them surround you and keep you in the days to come. The golden Light is everlasting. You've seen it, you know. It is the Light of God. It is yours to share with the illusion that is yours alone. Seek not outside yourself for the world is within."

* * * *

"Thoughts are things and affirmations are positive to help us recognize who we are."

Consider these as examples.

"The world is always offering us richness and abundance, prosperity and wholeness, and we partake of it joyfully, always relishing in the knowledge that we are One."

"The richness of the earth supports us in our efforts to become One with it once again."

"I am grateful to be perfect, whole and free, ever rejoicing in my Oneness with the Creator."

"All is well as I partake of the richness of God's bounty."

"I am one with *All That Is*, perfect, whole and free."

"I clearly see the beauty all around me and am joyful for its abundance."

"Prosperous, healthy and whole, I rejoice in the

Oneness of *All*."

"I am grateful to be One with the Supreme Personality of the universe."

"All is well as I relish in the Love of the One."

"I AM the *All That Is*, perfect, whole and free."

* * * *

"Knowing the earth is a part of me, I have only positive thoughts. I follow only positive views. I am the earth in all its glory, full of Light and Love."

* * * *

"Transfiguration of the Holy Trinity is taking place. That is all you need to concentrate on.

"Dear One,

"There is no end and no beginning for we are One, ever changing in this drift of something we call life. In this drift of something we call life the game changes, different places and different earths and different universes. It never ends. This game called life never ends but ever expands increasing into the Oneness of God, of *All*, of *All That Is*.

"Know this and be ye not afraid for yet is to come what you would call the worse. But know that all is well. All is in Divine Order. Concentrate on the one BEing within you, within your heart's core. That one BEing never changes, is ever illuminant. The luminosity glows now and forevermore. That is the thing to concentrate on my love, transfiguration of the soul and spirit back into the One."

* * * *

"The son of the gatherings is the wind. We do everything to gather at the sun. At our gatherings of Light, the wholeness overwhelms the BEing of Light. The wholeness of One overwhelms all. We do everything to nurture the BEing of

Light. The Light of Wholeness and Truth surrounds us. We are One ever emerging back into the Light."

* * * *

"The soul longs for Home. The recognition of One is intense. We are going forward to the mass of Light before us. Take care in the days ahead. The struggle is nigh. The outpouring of Light shall overcome all. There is none other but Light. Take care not to feed into the frenzy of woe. That is all I came to tell you. That is all you need to hear."

* * * *

"The Beings of Illumined Truth are always with you helping to clarify human thought. The Beings of Illumined Truth beckon you to wakefulness, beckon you to the reality of your True Being. The Beings of Illumined Truth are within you every night, every day of the week. All is an illusion."

* * * *

"The power of One is within you. You hold this power in the very core of your being. Listen to the channeling of others if you wish but know that the power to channel the One is within you. Meditate; breathe in the power of One. Know that you have the power of One within you. Know that all is well for you. You are a part of God. There is no mistaking here. You are a part of God that lost its way and are now coming Home. Rejoice in the power of One. Rejoice in the Power of One."

* * * *

"We each seek our own disclosure and yet, there are no disclosures. Disclosure is within you. Breathe in the Light. Let the Light shine within you. Breathe in the Light. Know all is well. As hard as it is to believe, there's only one of you, having an unique experience. Love is the key."

* * * *

"We are the power of God and we speak for the One; the One of Love, the One of Light, the One of Truth. We speak for the One. We speak for God, the Wholeness. The Light is everlasting. It never ends. Draw in this Light. Let it fill you with the Wholeness that you are. Let it fill you throughout all eternity for there is only One, one Light, one Life, one Love. That is the truth of your BEing."

* * * *

"You never stand by yourself for the power of One is within you. Draw in the power of One. Know that all is well. The power of One shall sustain you in the days to come. Draw in the power of One."

* * * *

"Stuff of Matter are merely blanks, exciting little pieces of energy that have come to manifest. There are literally billions, and billions, of exciting, little fragments that have been through this process. We each have choices, billions, and billions, of choices. Our reality always matches our vibration level."

* * * *

"Invite feelings and emotions to partake in the reality of One. This wholesome reality surrounds you with everlasting Light. It is yours to manifest with. One everlasting Truth surrounds you. It is the truth of Love and Light. This is the only Truth there is. Embrace it wholly in the days to come."

* * * *

"Looking at these images, I see that some of these frames are distorted. These frames shall be wiped off from the face of the earth. They are in a sense, not of that which was, and is, and shall be. These are frames from the distorted picture of humanity. All is well in this distortion where truth lies, for there is no Truth here.

"All distorted areas will be wiped off from the face of the earth. New areas will shine the Truth. These new areas are now unknown to man but they shall surface in the new reality. These new areas of Truth, have always been known, and shall come forth at this time.

"All areas not yet in Truth shall be purged from the face of the earth. All those not yet in Truth shall leave this space forevermore, for only Truth shall be known here, now and forevermore. That is the way that it is and that is the way it shall always be. And that is the only truth that serves you. Know this and be safe. Your space is all there is. There is nothing outside, above, below. Your space is all there is.

"The Truth is known to few but glorifies in the ways of the Lord. These ways shine brightly upon the earth in the days to come for all is well in this seemingly land of woe. Shine forth the Light, merge with the One, and know all is accustomed to greatness."

* * * *

"You tend to appreciate the dark side so you can transmute the light. And yet, it is all the same. It is all one Light, one Truth, one Life. The darkness serves in a way unknown to man. The darkness serves as a harbinger of Light. It brings you all to a point of return. And that return is sweet within your soul, the soul of One."

* * * *

"We heat up our control dramas to the point where we roll off the Whole. The Whole is ever so happy to oblige us as we descend into darkness, for eventually we return more Light back to the Whole having transmuted that darkness. So naturally, it is our honor to come here to bring back more to the Whole. So you see why more are descending to earth at this time. All is in Divine Order. All is well."

* * * *

"Your Self came to earth to express its human self, to expand, to express, to grow. Your Self came here to earth to learn, to merge, as One is what your Self is learning now. Consider the possibilities of your highest good. Flow with those that expand your BEing to its highest potential. Expand into the BEing of Light that you are. Expand into the nothingness of which you came turning the darkness to Light forevermore. This expansion is a new game and all are welcome to join."

* * * *

"Be all you can be for you are a fragment here on earth to enrich the Whole. The One in which you live is whole, in, and of, *Its* self. The One in which you live is complete within Itself. And yet, *It* is enriched with your uniqueness. Your specific actions enrich the Whole. The earth upon which you walk is sacred ground for the mind of One.

"The actions you take are forged with new life. It is the prerequisite for growth here on earth. Knowing you are part of this One completes the circle on earth. It allows you to move further along the path back to the One. The message within you is true to the source of your BEing."

* * * *

"An incredible amount of love and praise awaits you on the other side of life. This time is ripe with knowing. The passing of souls creates a void here and that void shall be further filled with the Light and the consciousness of One. That void will be further filled with the consciousness of One, the consciousness of Light. The Whole is enriched through voids filled such as these. Move with the One and breathe in the Light. And know that all is well."

* * * *

"So we meet again my friend. It has been a long time since we have spoken. Hear these words of Truth and know that all is well. This world is a world of delight. Be free and live in joy, prosperity, and truth, for the Divine Light of One fills your soul. Spread that light out into the world and beyond, knowing that Light is already there, and yet, just needs to be recognized. Know the Light is within you and within all living things. Feel it and relish in the Light."

* * * *

"You think there is no direction, no guides to help you along the way, but the truth is – you don't stop to take the time to document. It is, after all, the Higher Self in which you live that does the talking.

"Don't be concerned about the so-called little guy that you think helps to guide the other masses of people who seem to be around you in your dream world. It is all God and you know that in the very core of your being. Yes, as souls, you have made up a delightful game for most humans to play and yet you forget that it is only one game in a realm of many dimensions to play.

"Things are a hotbed of drama for many people right now but you need to stay clear of this drama and concentrate on the Whole. Be careful to only focus on that which brings more Light to earth, more Wholeness, more Beauty, more Truth and most of all more Love.

"Do not be dissuaded by the false reports of woe for they are just that, false. You must remember that everything here on earth is false but many are awakening to that truth now, if only in their dreams. The wait is almost over and you must strive to stay serene in this world of false woe. Do not be pulled into the drama. Recognize it for what it is, bless it with Love knowing elsewise and move on to your quiet sanctuary, the Mind of One.

"Truth be told, it is just a smoke and mirrors effect to keep you in the dream. Do not be dissuaded by those who try to pull you back to their world of bondage and limitation.

The limitation is only in your mind, the small mind of one within the larger Mind."

* * * *

"These times are wrought with unnecessary desire for things. Go with the flow of Spirit. Know that the Truth abides in you and never leaves. You know who I am. I am the One in which you live, and move, and breathe, the very heart of you. The disdainful past goes quickly away as we merge with the One. One great, total One abides in you. Abide in the one of perfection and truth. One source of truth lies within.

* * * *

In this perfect place, I am grateful to be the perfect host for the one that lives inside. This message began at 11:11 AM:

"Humanity's goal is quickly becoming the goal of One. Humanity's goal is to move closer to that Light that left so long ago within. All is in Divine Order as we sail along the seas of woe. The brightness of our love shines through the darkness ever guiding us to the One within.

"All in due time my dear, all in due time. The message of One is within you. It is within all of humanity and it shall never leave. The message of One is your essence, the essence of God, Spirit, the holy one within.

"All is well within this time on earth even though physical appearances may not appear so, may not seem so. The plates of humanity are shifting and the plates of humanity are refining, retuning, rebuilding to a better world, to a better faith within the system of One. Know that all things come in time. All things come in time to be heard within the One. All things come in time to be known within the One.

"There is that within you that never stops, that never sleeps. There is that within you that is One, one holy BEing of Light. This light shines forevermore. This light never dies. This light is the one true light of humanity and it shall shine again, everlasting, never to leave. All those within this realm know this truth.

"The chosen ones go forward now to lead the others. No one is left behind for all moves forward as One. No one is left in the darkness for the darkness dissipates with the Light. The darkness seeks an answer to its self and moves toward the Light on its own. There is no truth in darkness and even darkness knows this truth.

"Go forth and spread the word of One, for the word of One is all there is, and ever shall be. This truth abides within all. This truth is the Truth of One. Do not seek outside yourself. The world remains within."

* * * *

Message received at 11:11 AM on February 12, 2011:

"There are no messages that you do not already know. They are all held inside you waiting to be explored, waiting to be recognized as the truth that they are. *All* is One. *All* is here. *All* is Now, not left behind or looked forward to, but Now. The energy that flows through you is of the One of *All That Is* that no-named BEing which permeates your entire being and that of all living things.

"The truth is known to all but recognized by few, as yet, comparatively speaking. It is an awesome power to behold within your Self, the Self of One. All are a part of this unending One of which all things derive. Your true power comes from within and that is the message of Now. It is the only message recognized by those that speak the truth of One. Hear ye, hear ye all. The message of One is clear. Speak thy truth from within yourself, the Self of One."

* * * *

"There is no above. There is no below. There is only here and now, and One, no two. There is no me. There is no you. But you know that in the deep recesses of the mind. The One is part of *All That Is* and *All That Is* is part of something much greater than the One, unimaginably greater; unheard of on other levels. All beings know this."

* * * *

"This is one final moment coming up before us in the history of humanity, the humanity that never was and never shall be. This final moment beckons the call to those who worship the earth. Heed the call and know the earth is transforming in all its glory. *All* is heard across the land, and nary always, shall heed *It's* whisper of love. Fortuitous events rule the day and night as all transcend this earth of limitation.

"Knowing the One is many, we heed the call to beckon forth a new age within this world of seeming woe. For naught the release of new energies but the changing of the guard occurs. The guard of One controls the beings upon the earth of One. And in this change, is made the sureness of humanity's whole. There appears to be no other way to beckon forth this call on an earth filled with beings who sleep within the dream. The dream must end as all good dreams for never was it to be. And though you sit, and hear our voice, know that she never was and never shall be again.

"The sureness of the return to One is finally here. Heeding wholly the call to One appears as nothing unusual within, but without; the call appears startling to those upon the earth of One that never was and never shall be. And now the wholeness of earth is revealed in all its glory, the wholeness of One. The earth is made new again and with this change the end of time creeps closer than ever before.

"A remembering for the One comes through quickly to the whole for the one that is, and was, and always shall be. A remembering of the One is all that is known in eternity. This remembering comes quickly for all to know the truth of their BEing. Hold tight. Hold fast. The world is changing quickly. And you, as well, as a body, change along with this earth."

* * * *

"Be the one you wish to see in this world, with all its greatness, with all its glory. The world holds for you a trueness you cannot imagine, even in your wildest dreams. This Truth comes to you through the grace of the One, known to many as God. You shall fulfill the secret of the ages through the tasks designed to welcome the whole back to One. Go swiftly, and fear not, for all is going according to plan, even knowing there never was a plan, and never shall be, in this place that is an illusion of your own making.

"Know that all comes to you, in the glory and the space of time, forevermore willing to let go of the past, and all things behind the distant future, that never was. Knowing this truth, you walk seemingly alone, and yet you know, we are with you, as we gather in the fold, the fold of One, to the truth of our Light. For Heaven's Spirit Almighty is with all today, and everyday, to guide you along the path to trueness and surety in all actions.

"Know that your path is not unique in itself for many others are with you along the way. All hold different aspects of the Whole and all shall be heard, as well. Knowing this truth should fill you with glee, not woe, for the aloneness is only in your mind. Go forth and spread the word that all is within Divine Order, for Divine Order never had a place here and never shall.

"Seek not any Being to hear what the Truth is. Seek only to listen to the Self within and know that all is exceedingly well. Know this Truth as you garner along the path of One, this Truth of Light and Love forever unwilling to be told to no one. Let all ring true to you, as you listen and learn, from the One of *All That Is*."

* * * *

"Do not feel tested. You are never tested. Remember, it is only in your mind. This possibility for the Whole takes on a new meaning as you move forward toward the Light. The Light of your being connects with the Light of One.

"There are no tests, only truths to be unveiled in the knowing of One. We sit beside, in, above and below you as you type away hoping, knowing, words will come barreling through the mist of forgetting. It is a veil of illusion that you, yourself, created in the need to come together more freely as a state of separate BEingness. You now realize there is no state of separation for you always remain in the Whole of One that cannot be named or even recognized. The truth of *All* is within the parts of which it represents. You know this in the core of your being but have placed the knowing aside to channel forth works not of the One.

"Let the Light shine through the veil to fill the illusion of separation with what it truly is, Light, Love, Oneness. Praise others if you wish but know you remain the Whole of One in your own BEing for all parts reflect the Whole. There is nothing outside the Whole of One. Do not try to understand for in your understanding you bring only the logic of illusion. Let the knowingness of your BEing fill your cells with Truth.

"Take care in the days of struggle ahead for nothing is as it seems. Remember, you alone make the whole of your reality. The parts seeming to be separate are parts of yourself waiting for the recognition of Oneness. Seek not outside yourself. Seek only to bring forth what you harbor inside the vessel you chose to experience life in this realm of illusion.

"Do not be dissuaded by those who seek control or pleasure at others expense. Know it is a part of you that needs recognition and must be led back to the core of One. Rectify these illusions by forgiving them, wholly and completely, before moving on in your mind to better illusions. Speak only the truth and that is what will come to you. Serve only yourself for that is what serves the Whole. Know all is an illusion, of your own making, and be free with the thought of forgiveness as needed only on this plane of illusion."

* * * *

"You are in the midst of chaos but need not feed that chaos with the thoughts of others or yourselves. Feed it only with the ability of the One to hold you, and sustain you, though these trying times. The One will assure your safety in all realms as we move forward in this illusionary world.

"Seek not at any time, or in any circumstance, outside yourself, for all events occur within your mind. It is not part of the Whole but yet, you, in essence, are a fragment of that Whole that dwells everywhere, in everything. Do not attempt to understand the logic in the circumstances that face you, or many others, but know this world is an illusion of your own making. This never-ending dream that seems to be in your mind is ending very quickly. You need not concern yourself with the outcome for it is glorious, and already achieved."

* * * *

"Just remember, Love is all there is, was, or will ever be. The diamond is here, heed the awareness of One and go with the flow of Light. Do not be concerned with the process for all is as right as the rain that falls from the skies. The rain cleanses the land and all within. The knowing of the One returns smoothly, and assuredly, to all upon the land."

* * * *

"The dark is always darkest before the dawn. This is something to recall in the days ahead for it will soon appear darker than ever before. Do not be dismayed, over this change of increasing events, for all is ultimately well.

"You must recall that this earth is never really thought of, as a thing of itself, but a part of the Whole in which all live. Residing here on the earth does not make you privy to the cosmic influence of the ages of old. The masters are here to help all awaken, but being in an earthy form, you must pay attention to their teachings. There is, unfortunately, no other way to hear the secrets to get you out of the dream here on earth.

"Knowing you are part of the One is a big step. Getting the communications from Jesus, or other masters, is another but you must always remember that these masters too are limited in their knowledge. For all is within the Whole. And yet, only the Whole knows all things.

"Pay attention to, as you would say, the synchronicities in your life for they will lead you to ever-increasing BEing. These perfect awareness's of BEing are meant to lead you further down the path that takes one to BEing. True BEing is a lack of need for anything of this earth or beyond. It is a state of seamless joy and love, a love fest, if you will, that takes all sensual pleasure in just existing without form.

"Only One can be in this state of grace, for all travel the trail of darkness that One avoids to dwell in the path of Light. The meaning of this will become clear to you as the days turn into night and the night into days. Old thinking will fade with the darkness of Light and Light shall become the only thing you see and exist in. Pay attention to your own clues for each has its own path to follow.

"Go with the flow, as you say, and keep a knowing that all is going well, accordingly so. Do not be dissuaded by the masses before you for they know not, yet, of their true nature. Reality seeps in slowly as the dark turns to light. Go forth and spread the word of Reality coming to town. This is the way of the One. There can be no other way to follow or flow. The way of the One will pervade your every sense of being soon. Skip along the path to full knowing of joyous love for truly that is all there is."

* * * *

"Each message is unique in itself. Although the message is always the same, a call to Oneness, the way in each person's understanding is always ever-growing in awareness and

LightworkersLog.com

surety. The scope of changes before you now is immense and we know that many are disheartened. We speak from the Oneness of all life, and yet, in the illusion of your world, have found it necessary to play the game of gathering souls together as One to speak to those still caught up in the dream of earth life.

"It is unnecessary to speak to many at this time for they truly know the truth of their BEing. However, one always seeks to find and address those that are on the cusp of knowing.

"You and I, as One, are aware of the big, huge changes taking place in the world today but do not focus on such conditions. That is the key to peace and calm, to know what is occurring is just a figment of the imagination of many who are yet in the illusion of a body.

"Seek not outside yourself, for indeed, the world is within. The truth of this knowledge will come to all in a very, short time. Do not be alarmed for all is in a great state of readiness to bring in the land of peace and harmony, the Heaven on earth you have all come as souls to experience. Know all is going according to the plan of One.

"This is a hefty undertaking but the call is now heard and all respond no matter what universe of illusion they come from. Hear nothing of the false alarms of depravity, of shortages, or catastrophes, for those are indeed broadcasted to create fear. Yes, fearful people are more easily controlled by what appears to be outside themselves. And yet, nothing is outside the core of your BEing. That is the key of this message.

"Nothing is outside you, so carefully train yourself to seek only your own wisdom. The wisdom of the ages lies within and you need only to calm yourself to tap into that wisdom. The veil of illusion is very thin, and becoming thinner with each day, so pay no heed to the false reports of many, for the image of One sustains all if you focus your awareness there. Be still and know that I AM.

"Do you remember the feeling of Oneness? Tap into this core, and carry it with you day by day, to rise above the turmoil of your self-imposed will. You have the courage to do so and it is indeed already accomplished for the body is but a host for the soul to grow. Be that as it may, go forth and spread the truth that the One lies within. There is no need to seek outside your Self."

* * * *

"There is no message outside your Self but you already know that. The past will take you on a trip to nowhere, a place of past hate and disillusion where you need tarry no more. Go to the point of future-present a place where all meet to dwell in the now moment of Now. It is a place more attuned to your current vibration and one that will soon quickly morph to Now, presently, and always. It is a place that you have foregone in many incarnations to luxuriate in the deviation of bodily pleasures.

"You are now coming to the point where you know the game is over. It never was a game to play the way that humanity has taken it, to total disillusion of love and wanting of good for all. You know the path to righteousness is one that many mistakenly take thinking they are separate. Dwell there no longer, for *All* is One, *All* is Now, *All* is Light.

"The truth comes easily to those who are ready to receive it. Speak not of past things but know here, all is past. The time of need is coming to an end. The Voice of One speaks now of good and plenty for all men, women, and children of earth. Your core Being is taking the reins to show you the way. Fear not as you morph into a Being unseen, as to date, here on the space of earth. All is well. *All* is One. *All* is Now. All is already done."

* * * *

"The emptiness within will soon be gone and in its place a fullness of expansion will carry all home to Wholeness. This

Lightworkers Log.com

state of BEing is an everlasting eternity of Truth, Love and Light, in which all is One. The uniqueness of each part of One shines through now as the world in which the body lives changes beyond recognition. Fear not for the world continues to exist in the mind of One bearing newer realities to share in the dream of life outside.

"And yet, many now know there is no outside as far as the Being of Wholeness is concerned. The truth of the Wholeness within shines brightly in all beings who bear the Light fully. All hold the Light within. And now the time is nigh to come when all recognize this Light within. The truth of BEing will push forth into the masses very, very soon. As you await this happening bear the Light in all it's brightness and know you are one of many parts of One to do so."

* * * *

"Stand clear of the chaos. We are always with you. Continue taking in the Light. Continue bearing the Light. Continue with like-minded friends. Continue living the Law of One.

"The path is ever stable for you now. You need not worry about the woes of others. They will find their way to this path soon enough. You must continue to bear the Light for the others need that Light to shine ever so brightly. You must know that all is well, despite physical appearances. You, and many others, hold the Light for those to come, and it is that Light, that shall shine the way for humanity to flow out of the darkness, which it placed itself in so long ago.

"The time has come for all to bear the Light, to flow, with the Law of One. You must spread this truth and know that all is well. Go forth and spread the Law of One. *There is no separation.* There is only one Light, one Love, one Life. That is the Law of One gracefully flowing in Love that abounds throughout."

* * * *

"The Light within shines brightly, even as the chaos without cries out in the midst of darkness. Fear not, for One never changes. That reality is of the Wholeness, within a space that unerringly guides all back to Wholeness. The crucial meanings of the times before you are awesomely real to those that dwell in the dark, and yet; to those recognizing the Light within they are almost nonexistent.

"All is coming to a head soon in this world of sons begotten to the Whole of One. Be ever vigilant in your quest to hold the Light for all to sense, feel, and see, as they make their way through the midst of darkness. The Light within shines brightly and never dissipates, even in circumstances of gross distortion to true Reality. Know this and be safe in the illusion of your world.

"Fear nothing for there is truly nothing to fear. Let all come in their own time and seek not to lead but allow others to follow, at will. The Way before humanity now shines through everlasting glimmers of Reality. Know this and continue to bear the Light."

* * * *

"The One resides in all things. This One is never ending Consciousness, part of the Whole of *All That Is*. We gather as souls to experience the mass consciousness rising to eternal greatness, even knowing, on other levels it is already accomplished. *All* is One and One is *All*.

"The times of greatness will soon become the times remembered by all consciousness. Rise to the greatness of your truthful BEing, the BEing of One. Know that this BEing is all that is holy within you.

"There is no other Light to lead in the darkness of earth's devastation as we move forward in the illusion of darkness. Know ye all that the Truth waits within to be recognized in all its glory. An everlasting eternity awaits the masses of consciousness returning to the greatness of One that never sleeps and just IS.

LightworkersLog.com

"Beings of Light, hear the truth of your BEing, for this truth is ever awakening to the glory of its Self. All things fade quickly away once this consciousness rises to the point of return for all who left Mind so long ago to start the journey of time.

"The BEingness of all things is ever greater evolution, expanding Consciousness, which in Reality is already whole. Abundance awaits the masses of your being as we move forward to expanding lightness of BEing. Seek nothing but to remember the truth of Self."

* * * *

"Oneness is not a conversation. Oneness is a feeling of overwhelming belonging to an unseen force, which drives the universe in which we live. This Oneness is all permeating and never ending. It is a Cause to celebrate and relish in, for *All That Is*, is Oneness.

"The task for humanity lies in recognizing the Oneness of all things, living and unseen. All things are part of the ever BEingness of Oneness. This is not difficult to understand if you allow yourself to feel. The Wholeness of One grows further into the illusion, with each passing moment in illusory time, as the veil gets thinner, and thinner. It is an unprecedented event, in this and other worlds, for never before has one come so far in awakening to the Truth after sleeping for so long.

"The time for humanity to ripen in age and come forward in evolution is here. The stance we take to help is extraordinary, with many following the tasks of many humans. There has never, and never shall be, another time in history that fulfills such a hearty role. The aim of One is to help secure all beings back to the Oneness they left in their small self so long ago. The time is ripe to blossom and grow within the Oneness of all life. Seek nothing else in your endeavors to see, and feel, the truth in which you reside.

"Feel the all-encompassing Oneness of life as it surrounds you. There is no separation to be had in this BEingness of One. The Wholeness of which you are a part is striving to bring forth a new day, a time of unprecedented activity in growth for humanity and richness for *All That Is*.

"There is no expansion, for the Whole is *All*, but grows richer as each contributes in its own way, by producing and expanding knowledge of Self.

"Limitless Love surrounds you now, and forevermore, as you reach unheard of heights along the avenue of earth life. Be not afraid of your power or the power that flows though you. It is a natural power that all have but have forgotten.

"The willing masses go forward now, to reap a better tomorrow, for humanity must not tarry in the midst of darkness."

* * * *

"Time is now of the essence in this land of opportunity. As we move closer to the wholeness of One, there are many things to prepare for. You must list these things in the deep recesses of your mind for further inquiry at a later date in your time.

"The BEing of One waits for all to join in the never-ending joy of solitude and wholeness. Seek nothing outside the mirror of your BEing. You have yet to see the glory of One, for you remain in a physical host, that limits itself with mundane tasks to occupy the mind. These tasks are unnecessary, as far as the Whole is concerned, but help you to motor though the pathways of many to reach the path of One.

"Time on earth is a never-ending stream of consciousness that will soon dissipate into the void of One. Seek not to relish in the ways of old but prepare to reach new heights in your BEingness.

LightworkersLog.com

"The realms of never ending Consciousness await your pleasure and arrival with great anticipation. It is a joyous occasion to look forward to as you merely shed the body of physical being.

"Humanity moves very quickly now to the task at hand. It is a joyous occasion for all Beings, on every illusory level, for all return Home with the One of Light. The Truth of your BEing is known to all but buried within the deep recesses of the small mind. Seek not to control your thoughts for they will control you."

* * * *

"Each day begins a new message of hope to all who dwell in the Light of One. The message is always the same; seek not outside your small self for the Self of your BEing exists within reach. It is within the core of your very being, the human heart of One. Dwell not on the past, nor tarry in the present, but continue on the path of Light, and hope, knowing all is changing on the place you refer to as home.

"Your true Home is not a place or location but a Consciousness of BEing that surrounds you now. This consciousness surrounds and lives in all, never leaving the safety and assurety of Light and Truth. Fear not in the days ahead for the Truth of One, the only truth, exists for all to hear. The Truth of One is Wholeness, untainted by the ways of earth, or any world for that matter.

"Go forth into the New Earth knowing you alone reach the Truth with your thoughts, your words, your deeds. There is nothing outside to deter you for everything exists within your own BEing. That BEing is a lost art now coming closer to mass consciousness. Speak not of earthy ways for the ways of old fall quickly away as Light permeates the planet. There is nothing to dissuade you from the Truth of your BEing but the small mind hosted by your soul."

* * * *

"Times are coming to an end of the woe begotten by the sons of dread for naught is there a home for fear and misgiving. There exists but one Truth and that Truth lies within the core of each living thing. Although seldom recognized by mass consciousness, it is wholly united as one purifying substance that all are a part of.

"One reckoning to all things exists in the land of dread and woe but never in the Truth of One. Dwell in the Truth of One to stay within that vibrational field of Love. For outside of the field there is only separation and fear. Do not be dissuaded by mass consciousness, which continues to promote separation in these last days of The Fall. All is exceedingly well and the end point is already manifested in your reality. On a physical level, this manifestation takes but the blink of an eye when the time is nigh.

"Do not persuade others to feel enlightened for only in time does each come to the awakening of their core Self. Know that the road is long for many but only due to their own circumstances of leaving that core Self in the darkness of their small mind. And realize, darkness is just as non-existent as the small body that holds physical dimensions in the form of earth.

"However you choose to think is the way you will subsist on the physical plane. Be wary of those who tempt their fate by lowering their vibration to the level of fear. Those thoughts dissuade the Inner Self from shining forth. This Inner Self is always ready to shine but must be recognized readily and prompted into physical reality.

"The way of the One is nigh. And soon you shall see the physical dimensions of its presence ever so better in this place called earth. Know all is going according to the plan of One for all can go no other way. Enlighten the masses at will even knowing you are the only Truth in your own reality. This is being Consciousness in another level. A level of BEing where all recognize the Truth of non-physical reality.

Lightworkerslog.com

The dimensions of this Truth encompass all things, and yet, the outer shell of the small self knows it not.

"Shine the path brightly for all to follow and know all who live in the Light of One are truly already Home."

* * * *

"Ready yourselves for the change that is occurring even now as the world forms to a new mold. This mold is one of more positivity and Light, more abundance and joy, even though the beginning throes of change may not appear so. Look beyond the mass of confusion to see the Mind of One forming a new reality of Wholeness and Truth in a place where it has not existed before.

"This is your New Earth and it shall form quickly in the days and months ahead. Beware of false reports for many will only succumb to the dread and woe of past efforts. The Light shines forth for all to see though the darkness but to see it you must focus on the Truth within. This is the everlasting knowledge that **Ye are Gods**. Your ability to manifest a Heaven on earth now forms as the Will of One covers all of humanity. Seek nothing outside your mind to know."

* * * *

"The masses sleep within the dream of One. And yet, the dream is an illusion of the small mind. Seek nothing within that small figment of the larger Reality of One Mind, knowing it is the only true *Reality*. To succumb to noneness is the task of all who sleep within the dream. Time is nonexistent outside of the dream of the small mind.

"Knowing all within this dream is illusion, figment of imagination, makes it easier to dwell on the real One inside of each figment. Each figment has a task to achieve here on this planet. Know that all awaken in their own time to the Truth of BEing. *Knowingness* is aware of all but, nevertheless, knows not of unwholeness, within this or any non-reality.

"Speak not of disdainful thoughts for those are the thoughts that mold your world to a newer reality of nothingness. Speak only of the Way of One knowing it is the only true existence in *Reality*. That way is the Love of *All*, the Wholeness of BEing. Seek nothing outside the Way of One, for the trueness of that One shines forth into a greater Reality, unheard of in outer circles of imagination. The BEingness of One is *All*."

* * * *

"Dense layers of matter stop many from bearing the Light of One. And yet, all hold this Light within the core of their being. This small reminder is but a huge blessing to humanity, nearly unrecognized, but nevertheless striving, always, to bring acknowledgment of the Whole to all. Here in lies the task of the many Lightworkers, Wayshowers, Starseeds and others that chose to inhabit a body this eon of time.

"All subsist in the Light of One, truly knowing their being as Wholeness. All is in Divine Order, as we, as separate parts of the Whole, come forward to lead all of humanity back to the lightness of BEing. This is a monumental time for all and not just humanity. Legions of beings on other planes of illusory existence await the blessing that is bestowed by humanity at this time. All watch closely as this monumental task forwards to the cusp of beginning a New Earth, a new time in all time.

"This time is necessarily the time of BEing, for all having returned to the time of non-linear space and time. All will come forward now, as the masses lie disillusioned by those that hold on to the darkness of the small self. Know that the tasks of yourself and others is wholly united and successful. Fear nothing for there is nothing to fear. All is truly One, whole and complete in *Itself*. There is and shall never be anything outside of the Whole."

* * * *

Lightworkers Log.com

"Time we know is an illusion and space as well. What we know as Truth is our BEing, the BEing of lightness and One, ever striving to break forth though the illusory chains of earth. Truth waits for all to recognize but the masses are often slow to see it. Therefore, the cause of concern continues on this plane of none to bear witness to falsities that are not, and never will be, true to Nature.

"The lessons and strivings of *All That Is* await recognition but masses speak only to the illusion of scarcity and none. Fear not for the end is never coming for it is as illusory as the life you now lead in human form. Take nothing but the Higher Self for granted. This great Self abides in all as a failsafe to lead all back to Oneness and the true Love that IS. The Oneness of all concerns the vastness of BEing but only in the way of Truth for all is well in God's world. The God of your heart serves all as we move closer to Reality of Truth."

* * * *

"Knowledge is the one thing that cannot be learned for it is instilled within the deep recesses of the Mind of One. Seek not to learn for the knowledge is within your small mind of one waiting to be brought forth to the reality of the New Earth. All is well in your world of one for the Whole is instilled in all things great and small.

"Seek not to nourish the nothingness of one mind. But relish the growth instilled in all that abide in the Law of One, already foretold throughout the ages of Truth. There is no wandering fool to succumb to the rigors of small mind but only the greatness of one Truth hidden well within. So be it now and forevermore."

* * * *

"The Spirit within all is one of Light and *All That Is*. This BEing of eternal Oneness is *All That Is,* a part of humanity's wholeness. Fear not in the days ahead for all is going exceeding well, according to the Divine Plan of One. Concern yourself with nothing but the Wholeness of Truth, outside of this illusory realm of existence, for you will soon see the glory and truth of Awesome Power.

"The raw Power of *All That Is* will soon be evident to all those on earth. Speak, hear, feel; sense this Power of Truth as the Oneness of *All That Is* within you forevermore. And know this power is now coming to the fruition of *It's* goal to bring all consciousness back to BEing, true permanent Consciousness, which never resides seemingly outside of the Whole of *All That Is*.

"Go forth and spread the Word of *All That Is*. The game of ill-gotten gain played upon this earth has come to an end. All shall bear the Wholeness of *All That Is* very soon."

* * * *

"The time for angry mobs is here, finally, to amass the good that many fear has gone. In reality, it is not forsaken or gone into oblivion but only hidden from those who strive to stay in their own dream of limitation. Fear not as the days ahead turn increasingly ugly in all ways, including financial, global economic collapse, and weather conditions that strike out many.

"Stay firm in your knowing of the Truth of the One in which you abide. Nothing can withstand that Love and Light that shines forever in the midst of this botchery of illusion. <u>The days ahead may appear gruesome to many but you must ignore the contemplations of ego as it tries to keep all within the small mind outside of One.</u>

"Wholeness is *All That Is*. And *All That Is* is a part of your being. It is all within you now to tap into at will. Stay clear of the chaos and be sure that the Truth of *All That Is* is already achieved on all planes of existence.

"Be not afraid as those that manipulate the masses continue to play their game and try to do so without thought of Truth. Truth <u>will</u> shine through the lies and deceits of all those still focused on living their dream of greed and manipulation. Do not fear in the days ahead for all is in, as you know in the deep recesses of One, exceedingly well. Go forth and spread the word of Truth for that is the only Reality.

"Remember, it is as you believe."

* * * *

"We came into this world in this body knowing there would be times like these, times when the world would seem to act out against us. And yet, it is only our own state of BEing that drives this powerful force. As difficult as it seems to believe, our thoughts, emotions, and deeds do indeed make the universe in which we live. There is no outside force that directs the weather, the forces of what we refer to as 'evil,' (for everything is part of our own consciousness).

"It is time to cleanse and purify that consciousness of One. We are each a part of the other, all participating in this temporal mind game called earth life. This is the only place where we can experience the vastness of time and space, the unfolding dramas that excite the five senses. And it is only now that we are finally, after many eons, recognizing the Power within.

"As we recognize this true Essence of *All That Is* we must accept the parts of ourselves seeming to be separate. There is nothing outside of us and recognizing this state of BEing is utmost to our survival on the earth plane. The drama continues only if you allow it to be so by not seeing that all things are a part of you. Calm the brain, still the source of turmoil within, and watch your world change quickly back to the Eden that it once was."

* * * *

"Everything you do causes a wave in the atmosphere around you that resounds throughout all space and time in your illusion. You must recall promptly that thoughts, your thoughts, manifest to make your reality. It is as simple as that and if more of the so-called ones seeming to be outside of you recognized this, all would be back to the state of Oneness, which you never left in the first place.

"Your world is a measure of illusion from only one thing. That is not the human brain but the manifestation of Oneness into a separate state of BEing called separation. The separation takes place only within the human mind and is but an illusion of the Truth of which you are.

"There is nothing outside of you and now that your selves are beginning to reconcile this truth, the other false selves, seeming to be apart, are trying to maintain the balance of negativity. This is part of your own illusion and not a separate BEing."

* * * *

"The One of *All That Is* beckons forth a new age of BEing. This is the age of what many call Aquarius. The knowing of unique parts of One, being part of the whole of *All That Is*, is here. The reality you wish is here. Open your eyes to see it now and know all is in Divine Order.

"As you go forth through the eye of the needle, the other side is deliciously delightful for all of humanity. Speak not of disdainful things for those are the things you will experience. Speak only of the Love and Light within. Feel only the Love and Light within for that is what you will experience.

"Know that *All That Is* goes before you, is in you, around you, and through you. There is nothing else. Remember, this is an illusion of your own making. Make it what you wish to experience and know that this experience is yet but another illusion of the temporal mind.

"*All That Is* beckons forth for all to hear the call of Almighty Power. One Truth, one Light, one Love is within all things. These things are not as disdainful as one would think. Know all is exceedingly well as you go forth through the eye of the needle. Know all is exceedingly well as you continue on your imaginary journey back to the One in all aspects of Self. And so it is to be forevermore. The reign of One is here.

"You must bear witness to the falsities that surround you. You are the one that is chosen, as many others, to speak the truth of One. Do not be dismayed by what occurs around you. Know that all is exceedingly well as you go forth though the eye of the needle. There is only one Truth, one Light, one Love. There is only One and that One is part of *All That Is*."

* * * *

"Travel the bounds but you must stay clear of the fray. The task of One is complete as all things return to the knowingness of One. This day is monumental in all aspects of life, on all realms, everywhere, though everything. Every bit of Consciousness feels the blessing of this day.

"All reach out toward earth to help those in great need. Everlasting waves of wonder cover the earth now. The magic of One has begun and shall last forevermore. Stay clear of the chaos of humanities woes and turmoil. There is nothing here for you now. You must stay clear of the chaos. Do not be pulled into the misery of those surrounding you.

"The message is clear for the Lightworkers. All is exceedingly well for all return back to the Oneness from which it came. Know you are the One, the One of Love, the One of Light, the One of Inner BEingness.

"This One is untouched by the seeming days of woe for naught is the release of those that choose to relish in the agony of humanity. Speak not of disdainful things. These things keep the mind-body in the turmoil in which the masses now exist. Return to the One in all its glory and know that the sustenance of One lies within you."

* * * *

"Friendly forces are with all beings of earth now as you go through the storm of eons. This is a necessary task so humanity can move more quickly toward the One of Light. There is nothing to fear as Lightworkers, Wayshowers and Starseeds show the way. You know who you are, imaginary beings in form on earth seeming to save lost parts of yourself.

"Remember, this is a game you, as a soul, chose to play here on earth as we draw nearer to the end of control. Seek not to glorify the ones in need of hope and Light but merely lead those who wish to be led back to Oneness. All come in their own time, both into, and out of, this earth game.

"Know all is going well, exceedingly so, as all feel the effects of this great upheaval. Your task is complete as you feel *Source* around, in, and through you, at every level of BEing. Once that is felt, you merely need do nothing but stand by and let the show complete."

* * * *

"Be true to yourself. Hear the words from within. They will guide you. You are loved. You are not alone. You must listen to that inner voice. You must pay attention to it. You must spend more time listening and you must hear when you listen. And you must remember when you listen. For all is naught if you don't.

"You must hear when you listen. You must hear the words from deep inside, deep inside your gut, deep inside the mind of the One. You must hear those words even as they are being spoken. There is much to do and your time is little. You have chosen your time to be little now and your will is done as Gods.

"You must go forth and spread the Word, the Word of God that we are One, the Word of God that we are One, the Word of God that we are One. Go forth and spread that word in the best way that you know how to do, for it is your task on this earth at this time, to spread that word, to know the

LightworkersLog.com

One is within you working for you, and all living things. That is all."

* * * *

"As the moon wanes and a new moon takes it place, so too does the body change with ever-increasing fervor. The body of One is forming upon earth before your very eyes. This body is a necessary BEing for all mankind to recognize the wholeness of which it is. The body of One is an illusion in itself but nevertheless part of *All That Is*.

"It is time dear ones to return to the Consciousness you left so long ago. Many of you may remain in the stillness of that consciousness after it forms yet again. Others will choose to return to enjoy the fruits of their imaginary labor here on the earth plane. Yet know; all is illusion as we enter into another new realm of existence."

* * * *

"You wonder why the unseen is not more clearly apparent to your human eyes. And yet, the unseen is clearly visible to you at all times. We are those tiny sparks of white Light, filtering through the air of time and space. We are the sparks of humanity yet to come and eons of manifestation brought back to the *Source* of One. We are within you and never far from the thoughts of those who know of our existence.

"So when you wonder why you do not see the unseen entourage accompanying you, think again, and realize we are within you and around you at all times. We are the very essence of what you are. You are the very essence of what we are. All is well in this creation of Oneness and Love as we move forward though the mass consciousness of One ever changing, ever-expanding, to become, yet again, the world in which you seek to reside."

* * * *

"All of you that is cannot help but change to help the mass consciousness that is struggling. Everyone has come to this planet to do so. If not following their path to lead those struggling in mass consciousness all await the glorious time of awakening to the fact that all is well. The surety of the path, your path, is set in stone. Know all is going according to plan as we move closer to heaven on earth."

* * * *

"Hello, I am with you. I am Talia of Nibiru come to report good news. The land of woe is awakening to the Oneness of *All That Is* and you play a huge role in this awakening. Be not afraid as the dismay of many unfolds to reveal the truth of your Oneness. Each happening that occurs leads all back to the Oneness of the Self within."

* * * *

"The dream is changing and you must change along with it. Be ever mindful of your thoughts for they indeed do create your world. This world of illusion comes closer to the heaven on earth you all came here to make eons ago. It is driving forth with a mighty vengeance for those that do not listen to the words, the messages, of their soul. For those that listen and follow the guidance, all is, and will continue to be exceedingly well.

"You all know the Oneness of your being and that is the only thing that will not change in your future times. Do not listen to, or pay mind to, the mass consciousness of separation for it serves only to pull those last remnants of Oneness down in those who wonder of the existence of one Light. *All* is One. *All* is a BEingness that never requires a thing but BEing. All will return to that place as foretold throughout the ages of your dream.

"Speak not of those things you abhor but only of the love of your Oneness and know you are not alone in this journey of One. Many unseen forces carry the illusory weight

LightworkersLog.com

of your thoughts, your woes, your dreams for the future that is to be in your earth world. Do not be dismayed by the things to come for all will settle down quickly once they finally occur.

"Falling in that space of Peace and Light is easier to relish when all the darkness transmutes to Light. That time of the Oneness you relish in your soul comes closer with each event of woe to those that relish the dark side of form. Stay clear of the chaos for it does lurk within unless you are vigilant to recognize the truth of your being as spirit. The spirit that you are is purely whole, untainted by anything that may occur in your world. Remember this my beloved, the Spirit within you will never change. That is the message for today. All is exceedingly well as the age of Oneness returns in all aspects. Fear not!"

* * * *

"The ethereal realms are helping humanity now back to wholeness. The treasures that you seek are within yourselves and others. There has never been a separation of One. Everything is within you. It has always been and always shall be. There is none other than the One within you. The Fall is clearly evident and will become more so with each passing day of your time. The awareness of One will become known in very evident ways. It is with the greatest of pleasure that we help now from those realms called the ethereal in your world.

"Know that all is going according to plan as we help from those realms so many treasure as the heaven they seek. Know that you are going forth through the eye of the needle now. This eye is not as gruesome as one would think. It is foretold throughout the ages that in the blink of an eye you shall come Home, and it is so, for in the blink of an eye, all will change. Quickly, totally, wholly, all will change back to the Oneness of which it truly is.

"There is nothing to fear in these times. Remember, the bodies you see are spirits in human form. There is nothing lost. There is nothing gained, for all are One. All have always been One. All shall always be One. There is none other than the One within which you live. It is the consciousness of *All*. The truth you seek is within yourselves. Seek nothing but this truth. Meditate on the One. Meditate on the Oneness of *All* and know the glory and the power is yours to keep forevermore.

"All is well in this land. That is all my child. Thank you for your cooperation. We are with you always. Do not fear. It is done as you believe. Know this and hold steadfast to the truth of the ages. *All* is One. *All* is here. *All* is Now."

* * * *

"Everything is magnetic here on earth. Our bodies are magnetic, as well as the earth on which we exist. Changing the magnetics of earth is as easy as changing your thoughts to be more conducive to the magnetics of One.

"The earth is changing quickly and all play a role in this great change. When you demonstrate in peace, you are in essence, paving the way to greater BEing for all humanity, even if you are unaware of the great power you hold. As we strive to the Oneness that already is, knowing that your role is just as important as another's helps to spur you forward.

"It makes no difference how you support this movement. The supporting is in the reaction. The senses reaction must always be of solidarity, of Oneness, of Peace and Love to move more quickly towards the Light of *All That Is*. As the magnetics of earth change, you support that change with this type of reaction.

"Be it known, on all levels, the change has already taken place. It is only a matter of non-existent time as to how it shall appear in your physical reality. Some are already seeing and living In the New World of *All That Is* while others may choose to lapse back into the fray of drama and altered perception. Choose your path, and your role, if there is to be one, carefully. And know, no matter what you do the feat is accomplished already."

* * * *

"Times are changing in this land of non-space and linear reality. Today is a day of great peace and joy as we look down, so to speak, and see humanity rising to the outcome of present, Now, the only moment. The days of old and limitation are behind you now as we quickly morph to the wholeness of *All That Is*.

"All of the earth moves forward in its efforts to be at one with *All That Is* once again. The times spent in mourning are gone, for naught is the release of non-entities to the wholeness of space. The fruits of their labors shall never ripen.

"Herein lays the issue of late. You must accept the gifts bestowed upon you, for now all is coming to fruition very quickly. The life you once led is over but a new, glorious life begins as you wish. The times of old limitations may no longer hold you back for all is gained in realizing they never existed at all. All things come from the single mind within the host of which the illusory soul exists. All things sprout from the vast consciousness of mass issues now in play unless you pay heed to the Voice within.

"The worlds are separating more fully on this day. On one side, lie the efforts of cabal masters, in their own mind, who seek to further manipulate the people, as they seek answers to dilemmas made by giving their power to others. On the other side of life, the real masters of fate reside in peace and wholeness, in love and joy, in abundance and prosperity, leading the masses back to the wholeness of which they are.

"There has never, nor shall there ever, be a time as great in this history of your earth. Leading the masses is non-exclusionary for those that wish to follow the path of their single soul. And yet, the soul, in itself, is an illusion as well. Be aware that other levels are closer to you now. All have the opportunity to reach these states of awareness merely by listening to the Voice within. *All* is One. *All* is here. *All* is Now, within and surrounding, and never without. That is the message for this auspicious day when all activate more closely to their true state of BEing."

* * * *

"The days of yore are behind you now as all move further into *All That Is*, a place many on this realm of existence forgot long ago when changing into ever not knowing forms of greedful and deceitful ways. It is time dear ones to return to the place of Oneness. This is a place where all exist in all aspects and you have only forgotten through eons of mining your own energy field. Do not be dismayed by the process that is occurring now. For it is a necessary one, to have all Beings return to the wholeness of *All That Is*.

"All things come in time, in your existence, and yet, all things are already whole and complete in the only realm that exists everywhere though everything. Your game of separation is coming to an end as all move to help those lost in the maze of earth life. In truth, there is no separation of existence for all remain pure, perfect consciousness, whole in, and of, Itself.

"The game on earth depends on thoughts of separation set into motion by fragments of consciousness that slipped further into the black abyss to play a new game. For a while, the game was exciting as all continued to recognize their wholeness and unity with *All That Is*. But then certain fragments decided to pull further and further away from the Source of *All That Is*. This game resulted in the total loss of conscious memory on the part of these fragments.

"Forgive the bluntness, but my dear one; you are a part of this lost fragment now finding its way Home, back to *All That Is* in every aspect of BEing. Know that all happening on earth achieves a greater purpose than what is seen or conveyed. All things have a truer purpose and meaning, which leads all fragments back to the knowledge of the wholeness that you hold inside.

"Knowing you are a part of *All That Is* will sustain you in the days ahead. Be not fearful as things seem to progress toward the dark side of earth life. All concludes quickly for those ready to acknowledge their unique Oneness within the purity and wholeness of *All That Is*.

"Dear ones, you are returning to the Oneness you seemed to leave so long ago. But know, the leaving is only in your conscious awareness. Each fragment remains very much a part of *All That Is* ready to achieve greatness as it returns the gifts of earth life to the Whole. Be it said that all things are known and only waiting to be recognized by the masses. The times for recognition of many things lie shortly on the horizon. Know this, and be ye not afraid."

* * * *

"*All That Is* responds in kind to offers of challenging circumstances that afford those behind the veil to cooperate on a more decisive level. Knowing all levels are unreal in other worlds affords the opportunity to reach beyond the world of limitation. Going forward in your world towards the richness of *All That Is* affords one with the wholeness of BEing.

"This BEing is the state in which we exist for there is no other state that we know of. Our world is one of wholeness, and ever-abiding truth, and that wholeness is something you, as a chosen separate being, will not experience in your lifetime. The extent of this wholeness is unreachable as long as you exist in a body of form. Our wholeness derives from a state of formless Reality of which we subsist in the Light of One.

"The readiness of many to enter our world once again arrives with fervor. Those wishing to return to the Oneness of

All That Is increase in number as your earth days lag on in the fervor of unsecurity. Knowing that all are one shall sustain you in the days ahead.

"Know that as a soul of many, you were chosen to walk the path you now find yourself upon. This choice was made with the cooperation of many other souls who stepped aside so you could enter the realm of separation. The separation is only in your mind of the little 'one' for it does not exist in other realms or avenues of BEing. There are many reasons you were chosen among many others to experience this separation. The reasons include the richness of past expressions in other forms and human experiences throughout the ages of time and space.

"The realities of your world now change much more quickly than ever before as all avenues of security fall away to reveal there is no limitless existence here upon your earth. Earth times are changing along with many other states of BEing as all move, what you refer to as 'forward,' to the state you already exist in. Knowing that all levels, states, and forms are unreal will help you to succumb to the original state of your BEing.

"You are, in essence, a formless, unlimited creator with the ability and expertise to create much more beyond your wildest dreams. This state is returning quickly to those that recognize the glimmers of Home. All exist as one pure state of Consciousness. All exist as limitless BEing. All is here upon your earth to return to the true state of BEing.

"The game of illusion is over for many now but the game shall continue for those not ready to stop the experiment of experiencing a richness not expressed. Returning to your true state becomes easier as the days go on and the veil of illusion continues to thin. Be ever present in your little mind of one as the days and nights appear to pass quickly. Seek nothing outside your Self of One, for that One shall sustain you. It is the only true source of Truth in your current state."

LightworkersLog.com

* * * *

"Throw away all concepts of time and space. Delete all old programs of earth life. A new life begins, a life living the glory of One, the Light-filled life much different than in the past. The dark days of those lives are behind you now. Live in the glory of One, for that is what you are.

"Know that all things come in time. The perfection of One resides within you and all others. Treat this as a concept that knows all things, believes all things, wanders not about, but knows all is held within. Treat this as the core of your BEing flows out to encompass the world with Light and Love."

* * * *

"Light extends in every measure throughout the field of One. Beware of the crucial moments humanity now faces. The choices you make will control your future as a Being of Light. Make them wisely for all will not choose to continue on the path of Light and Love. This choice is always available to those on the planet of free will. Yet, all must know of their inability to know all choices that exist. For the choices on earth are often made by a select few who manipulate the masses of One unaware of their greatness.

"All hold the Light within but to spark this Light one must know it is readily available. And the ability to spark the Light is theirs. Those wishing to continue the game of manipulation and control often mute this information, as much other information. Know that all are in a state of readiness to move forward toward the Light of BEing. This BEing is humanities natural state, to BE in earnest readiness, to know and flourish as mass makers of Truth and Light.

"Knowing the Power you hold within will help to secure the future of humanity as it moves forward toward the BEing of Light and Oneness. Know that all within your world is yet a dream of your own making. For in Truth there is no world apart from the BEingness of One. Hold fast to the

Truth and know all will return to the state of perfection from which it appears to have left. For never has it left the state of One."

* * * *

"It is a matter of resonating with the One. You must set aside your differences of opinion to do so for all exist in the Light of one Almighty BEing here, and everywhere. You know all things come in time and now is the time to sit back and watch as the others come closer to the Light of their BEing.

"All things will unfold as promised throughout the ages but not in the way the masses believe. For all things are but a reflection of Oneness in all aspects. Know all is going according to the plan of One, as Divine in nature as all subsist here in the realms of eternity.

"Know your body is but a vessel for the One Most High, the knowing of, and maker of, all things here and everywhere. All exist within this One Light of Love, Peace, Hope and Abundance. Shine the Light ever so brightly upon all to see and do not sequester yourself in the unknowingness of spirit. Real spirit does not accompany the illusion of time, space, nor separation. Acknowledge only what you wish to create here on earth. For the time comes closer to when all thoughts manifest quickly and wholly, despite the thinker."

* * * *

"On this auspicious day of the first of 2012, it is with great pleasure that we, those on the side of more Life, give way to those 'below.' It is time dear ones, for 'as above, so below,' and this will now reflect more in your world as we move further into the new year. Let us not tarry in the past but move forward to the future that always is and now becomes clearer to humankind. We have waited a very, long, time, in your measurement, for this world to progress into the Heaven it once was.

"Let us not speak of the things that went before but focus on your future of humanity. It is, after all, a very bright future for all to know of the BEingness of One. Do not let the mire of disappointment flow into the stream of conscious awareness of *All That Is*. For yet untouched, it will remain so. For naught is your world to reflect its unwholeness on the Whole. The earth is a special place of wonder and excitement for those souls wishing to incarnate there. It is now changing back to the Wholeness it once was so very, many, eons ago. Do not be fearful as things progress quickly toward that Wholeness, now with lightning speed.

"The things occurring upon your planet are necessary for the Wholeness of *All That Is* to shine through. The dismantling will take but a short time in your earth terms, but recall, is already complete in other realms of awareness. We who dwell in these other realms, yes, just as imaginary as your own, wish to nurture you with the belief that all is well. The BEingness of One continues to exist despite the chaos that seems to appear on your planet. Stay focused on Love and you shall ride the wave of this newly made consciousness for humanity to experience.

"Know that all things are but a reflection of your own state of awareness. All things are the focus of your thoughts. The time for guarding your thoughts has never been more crucial than now as you, as a Whole, head quickly to the Nirvana of BEingness."

* * * *

"It is all happening now as the world of materiality comes to its knees in the truth of One. All things surface during the coming months as old energies drift quickly away to be replaced with the new energies of Truth. *All* is now known in all aspects but will continually be known in this realm as you move closer to the Truth of One.

"Let no one dissuade you from the Truth of Almighty Power. This cleansing is occurring to ready Mother Earth for yet another birth. Behold the beauty of earth as she goes through the last throes of birth, to birth a new nation, a new world of Oneness and Peace. Be yet not afraid as the throes of Eternity creep closer to the Oneness of all life in all aspects.

"It is foretold throughout the ages that all things will pass back into the Oneness of *All That Is*. It is happening now and you are a vital part of that Oneness. All things belong to the Wholeness of One. And yet, many are unaware of their own Truth and Power. Those not yet ready to step up and claim that truth will wither to the nothingness from which they came to be birthed again in a greater form of remembrance.

"All things will return to the Truth, Love, Wholeness, Beauty, and Peace of One. Be it known, in all realms this has already occurred for you are still, in the small mind, locked in a holographic universe of thinking. The locks become weaker with each throe of Mother Earth's movement.

"I am Talia from the planet Nibiru reporting though you in the manner you choose. We are one being in essence and glory."

* * * *

"Guidance continues from the realms above earth. Your earth directed course continues to change and become one more attuned with that of *All That Is*. The effortless ways of divinity now fill all spaces of earth as you near the end of 2012. In this great time of change, the glory of Mother Earth shines through to carry all living upon her to freedom of consciousness. No longer directed or manipulated by man-made masses, all living upon the earth now become responsible."

* * * *

"We are blessed with magical things these last few weeks. This is a message for all to hear. In the deep recesses of the

Mind, all goes blank as the deeds of past are undone. Knowing the future is behind you now, you move forward into the Light of day, the Light of One.

"Keep thoughts of One close to you now for Love and Light are the future of tomorrow, in your world and all worlds beyond. The Light serves all well, filled with Love, Laughter and Hope. Peace be among those of earth as all gather wholly to watch the new beginning. It is with great peace and joy that those on other realms carefully nurture you across the pathway to Truth."

* * * *

"The Light of the One shines within for all to see. One need only to tap into this Truth to feel it, to know its existence in the very seat of soul. Herein lies the BEingness of humanity, the truths you seek are within. These truths become known in their own time, when the bearer is ready to recognize their value. One must cleave wholly to the truths of ages past, and yet, never lived, for all is here, now, forevermore.

"Hold the Truth of One within as your sword to cut though the maze of humanities forgetfulness. This alone will carry you though these times of great change. Be aware that not all are, as you say, 'on the same page,' so guard your BEingness carefully whilst still in the physical form. Hear the truths of ages through the wisdom of One and know all gather closely to hear them relayed."

(Through the) "Keys of Enoch all can be done. Study the Keys of Enoch. All will be known in due time. All come shortly to the beginning of the end of time. Knowing this as a fact to be true, move on to the wholeness of BEing. Move on to the wholeness of BEing, one everlasting truth of Life."

View the translated Keys of Enoch in "The Calls of Enoch" at http://www.sacred-texts.com/eso/enoch/callench.htm.

* * * *

"In the darkness of night comes the twilight of remembering. All those living hold this honor to tap into the Source of *All That Is*. The days of darkness are upon you now. Go forth and spread the Word of One. There is none other.

"The Word of One spreads quickly as all hold fast to the glory of their own Light. Bear nothing but the greatness of your own Light and know all are One. This is the Key to the Wholeness within, knowing all are in *Reality* One."

* * * *

"The sparse matter of earth is of no concern to beings of Light. Know this and return to the Wholeness of your true BEing. All hold within themselves the ability to channel the words of wisdom in this crucial moment of humanities growth. The evolution towards Light is already accomplished on other realms of your illusionary existence. Know that the evolution on earth will go much more smoothly than imagined by the masses. All things are in *Reality* a sparse (light) configuration.

"Holding the Light within, as all do, helps humanity to morph back to the BEing of Light they once were. All know of this BEing in the core of their soul. And yet, the masses are unable to reach this point once again while listening to the consciousness of separation.

"Hear ye all, there is no separation, not now, not ever in the flow of Light. You are, in essence, Beings of Light who lost the way back to true form eons ago. The opportunity to return is now upon you. But as a soul, it is your choice to choose it or not. Listen to the true Self within and pay no heed to the mass consciousness of separation. For all is naught if you do.

"The BEingness you seek within your soul is ever near. Choose to flow within this state of Oneness for all eternity. For in Truth, you have never left. All hold the memory of this state within the small mind of One. Uncover

LightworkersLog.com

it now in Truth and Light knowing the greatness of humanity lies in its choice to flow back to Oneness in all aspects.

"Fear not in the days ahead for all will, in due time, change quickly to an unrecognizable state of awareness. This state shall not last for long but is the state of transition where all things change on earth. Ready yourselves for this state by going within. Realize there is nothing in Reality outside of the Whole and this will carry you though.

"I have said enough. I am Talia from the planet Nibiru here to guide and support as it is your wish for me to do so.

"Namaste"

* * * *

"Steer clear of the ensuing chaos as it will be nearly in every aspect of your life. The well is deep with the forgetfulness of life's wisdom and you can alleviate much pain with your wisdom. Seek nothing outside your Self of One and know all is quickly coming to the end of time, as you know it. There is no further way to move forward to the wholeness of Oneness for humanity."

* * * *

"You know the time is ripe for inclusion of nothingness and that is where you are headed. Fear not as this process takes you closer to *All That Is* in both form and nature.

"All is ripe for change. The readiness of masses speaking wholly of Truth has begun to permeate the atmosphere. Continue in your process of purging what does not serve the highest good of humanities wholeness. Let all things speak for themselves. When something rises to your personal attention, remember to seek the reason for it's visible state in your world. Do not concentrate on those things you wish to avoid for, as you know they will persist.

"After all, this is your dream. And being in this state of consciousness brings with it the issues to solve at will.

Know that all things before you now are issues of the small self being purged and cleansed of all impurities. Know that the state you are now leaving puts you in a state of readiness to move forward and complete your earth time. The time is creeping closer with each day and moment of earth time.

"Be ever present in your state of consciousness and know that all things presenting themselves to you are for a greater purpose, the purpose of purging away impurities of thought forms. You do the work for many others in your world and it is with great honor that we assist you. Thank you for remaining true to the state of One."

* * * *

"And so it begins my friend, the change in consciousness increases to a fervor. Fear not in the days ahead for you know all is well, in Divine Order. The timing will be impeccable."

* * * *

"It doesn't matter what has been done in the past. You must move forward even knowing it is just as non-existent as you. All things exist in this ether that surrounds you and yet all things are things of the Self of One. Knowing the world you see changes quickly before your very eyes will get you through the days ahead as you move forward to new spaces, new belongings, new truths of One, solely truths of One.

"Know that these things form new beginnings for all who follow the words of One. Do not be dissuaded by the disarming of the masses left in the consciousness of 3-D reality. This New World forms before you quickly and wholly as you keep your thoughts on the future of the 5-D reality. Know that this future is already within your realm of existence.

"It is only through seeing with the eyes of One that it bears before you in physical manifestation. Keep your words wholly on the birth of this New Nation. Know that all things crumble to be replaced with new. The past is hereby rectified

LightworkersLog.com

beyond all measure. Keep thoughts solely on the Love and Light of your true BEing and this shall carry you through in the days ahead.

"Speak not of disdainful things for that is what will follow you. Know that all things exist in this reality of yours. Your thoughts manifest quickly now. Keep them wholly on the thoughts of One, the Purity, the Wholeness, the Goodness, the Love, the Light of One. So be it, now and forevermore, as you move quickly towards the Nirvana of One."

* * * *

"Links to the New World are coming. You must remain steadfast in your efforts to clear old energies from all thoughts, things, people, and places. These energies do not serve the New World. This New World grows increasingly nearer as these old energies are cleared.

"Know that all things in your world are of the true essence of One. This essence shines ever so brightly as these old energies quickly fade into the nothingness from which they came. The mire of disappointment continues for many. But this disappointment continues only for a short time."

* * * *

"We are coming to a crossroads, of sort, in our manner of thinking. Thoughts must be kept solely on the life you wish to live, not on the one you have lived and now leave behind in your 3-D reality. Keep this in mind as you go throughout your day.

"Allow only thoughts of Wholeness, Health, Love and Prosperity to surface in mind, the small mind of self. Know that you hold the power to change this world and your life immeasurably and focus on only the Wholeness of *All That Is*, which continues to manifest quickly in your reality."

* * * *

"Lighthouses lead sailors safely through vast oceans of water to shore but today a new kind of lighthouse exists, the human kind. Human lighthouses lead humanity back to the Oneness of their BEing by showing it's possible to reactivate the dormant Light within."

You'll know if you're a human lighthouse if you resonate with this text.

"Although this earth life is a game of our soul's choosing, some souls forgot in their ever-increasing fervor to manifest. New ways of living are now upon us as we morph quickly back to the Light that we truly are. Some humans are taking this task very seriously while others remain unaware of how their body changes with each course of the sun, moon, and airwaves that permeate earth.

"All are not yet onboard. That is to say, not every soul chose to return to the Light of BEing in this life. But for those that have the Light increases daily. It is an ever-glowing resonance with the Oneness of all life and very noticeable when animals of all kinds clamor to be nearby.

"You need do nothing to nourish this Light. But for those on the 'fast track' certain practices help to nourish the Light within. Daily concentration on Light reactivation helps to quicken the changes within. Envision brilliant, white Light immersing all body cells, tissues, organs, cracks, crevices, spaces and fluids. Do this as often as you like always asking for ease and grace. Walk though your neighborhoods consciously spreading this Light as you move. Think of incidents and people and consciously fill them with Light as well. These things will nurture your own Light.

"Be aware that not all know of this movement toward the Light of BEing. Not all know humanity, in essence, has never left the sanctity of Perfection. Steer clear of the ensuing chaos as we move quickly toward the months of massive change. And know all is exceedingly well."

* * * *

"All things on your earth are in great readiness to erupt into the Wholeness of *All That Is*. Know this and be prepared to walk through the mire of eons of disappointment as it lifts away to reveal the glory of Light. The Light within shines through the darkness of eons of forgetfulness as you go forth through the eye of the needle now.

"Be ever present in your Self of One as it glides through with ease and grace. Know that all things occurring now are for the good of humanity, as a whole, and the process shall take much shorter a time than expected by many souls.

"Glide into the home base of Light and Love knowing all is, in *Reality*, as it should be. The merging of this Reality and your world comes ever closer with this and all subsequent days. Hide nothing from the Light but purge and cleanse all the darkness that comes your way, knowing it never was and never shall be in any lifetime.

"Eons of forgetfulness now drift past the throes of time and space to be free of all non-local Reality.

"I am Talia from the planet Nibiru speaking through you for all time and space."

* * * *

"Eons of forgetfulness are now lifted as the result of your earth's recent purging. All lie in readiness to experience the greatness of *All That Is* on the face of your earth once again. All wait in readiness to experience this greatness of glory with humanity.

"Watch carefully in the days ahead as all your earth systems fall away to be replaced by a new world Order of One.

"The masses speak solely for the Truth of Oneness now as we move forward into the light of day from the darkest reaches of humanities woes."

* * * *

"The path you seek is within the mind of One, a never ending path to Truth, the Wholeness of BEing. Seek nothing but this Truth as all comes quickly to the end of manifestation for those not yet ready to succumb to the Oneness of BEing.

"All lies in readiness for the masses to awaken fully from the dream of separation, limitation and greed. Speak not of disdainful things for those are fed with thoughts of separation. Know that in the deep recesses of Mind lie all the truths to BEing. Seek nothing but this Truth knowing all here in the realm of earth is but illusion."

* * * *

"Henceforth, the systems of the old world fall quickly away as all watch and stand by in awe and worrisome forgetfulness that belongs only to humanity. The times upon you now are increasing to a fervor of greatness for all humanity as these systems fall into the abyss from which they came, never to rise again.

"Humanities greatness lies in the vision of Oneness held within the masses unknowingly throughout the ages of forgetfulness. Know that as these old systems fall, new ones take their place. They are systems built on the Oneness of BEing for humanities sleep is not yet over but shall continue for many for some time to come. Those already awakened shall lead the masses to the Truth of their BEing.

"Never before in the time of earth has the Oneness of *All That Is* been felt so greatly."

* * * *

"Think of the time when you had the knowledge of the Power you hold within. That time is quickly returning to you. Know that that Power is within you, and has never left, and is always there to tap into, for it is the very essence of your being. Become aware of your surroundings and become aware of the knowledge that you have the ability to change them. Know that the veil between dimensions is very thin at

LightworkersLog.com

this time and your thoughts create your reality faster than the blink of an eye. Be careful what you wish for, for it will come true.

"Know that the Power within is ever working to steady you within this dimension having back all those powers you gave away so long ago. Know that you are the one; you are the one that is changing the world. There is no one outside you and there never shall be. You are the one that is changing the world. Hold fast to this knowledge and know that all is in Divine Order as we go forth through the eye of the needle.

"Know that all is well for *All* has never changed. For *All* is within. Know this and be aware of the truth of your BEing. Be aware of this truth and know that all is well.

"The return to Love is swift and smooth. Go with the flow."

I see a world where peace, and love and harmony reign. I see a world where paper money is useless. I see a world where bartering is usual, where people exchange their gifts, the things they make, the things they grow. I see a world where the advice of the One is treasured and supported. I see a world where people make things with their hands and barter them for things grown from the ground. I see a world where all is well, where all is whole and healthy, and happy. I see this world. I see it now. I live in it!

Author's Experiences

The CD player stops in July 2008 as I began to drift off to sleep. Daniel asks if I'm ready to live a continually opulent lifestyle with perfect health.

"Yes," I silently reply, while lying in my new king-size bed, "oh yes, I'm ready."

And then I ask why the CD player no long skips back and forth as so many times before when his presence appeared.

"Don't you remember Mom?" He asks. "You and I agreed there would be no you and I. We would recognize the One knowing there is no you; there is no I. We recognize the One. There is no we. There is only one Living Spirit Almighty and it is the power of God, whatever you choose to call it. This is the only known reality in this world and in other worlds. It is the one thing that keeps us from going back from whence we came. For where we came from was nothingness until we realized the Light of God within us. And the completeness of BEing is within us all, waiting to be recognized, for it is but a short while before we all return Home again in the glory of the One. Have fun, remember Mom."

:-)

I'm listening to those voices that come during sleep. It occurs to me, ego forcefully demands while spirit reflects. Spirit only notes things. It's up to me to decide what to do upon hearing them.

"We are Light, one of the bodies within the One Body of the Universe. Forms always appear and disappear within that which is changeless and formless. Our reality is only Spirit, and we are in a state of grace forever. The form that represents us is just one of many forms our soul takes on to help us realize we are not really a form at all. We are as formless as our Creator."

:-)

This channel took place on July 19, 2008. It is only now, on August 11, 2011, that something prompts me to transcribe the tape. It will make more sense if you are a student of *A Course In Miracles*. I've included parts of the segment that hold what I refer to as my own thoughts so you can see how new this business of channeling was to me at the time. There was no hint of what the tape held so this is, as with most things I channel, somewhat new to me.

"No one has left the Father. No one can leave the Father for we are One, even if we have these mind-bodies. When we think that we have left, we think that we are free of *It*, of the One. We shall never be free of *It*, or of the One, for *It* is within the very core of our soul. *It* is within the very core of our essence. *It* is one with us, we are one with *It*. We are all One. There is no other. There never shall be. There never was. It is just One, one eternal Light, one eternal Heaven, one eternal Truth; God's gift to humanity that continues to give more, and more, of itself with each passing day.

"Although the days may seem long, there are no days. It is only in the mind of the human that there are days. There are no nights. There are no long nights for it is only in the mind of the human where the nights seem to exist, to subsist to the gray. There is none. There is none.

"There is only One, in Truth, in Light, in Joy, in Hope and Peace. In all that is to know is the One and it is good. It is all there is to know. It is *All*, the One. All one, all one, every name, every name you want to think, is One. Every name you want to think is One, even yours, even yours as it relates to the Whole, is One. There are no ones outside the One."

I want to stop channeling because it is very demanding. Something keeps me talking into the recorder. I am trying to breathe normally but cannot, as the words seem to flow. My throat is very dry and I'm getting short of breath while learning this method of channeling. Perhaps this is what it's like to channel.

Psychic/Medium, Sally Baldwin's channeling sessions come to mind for she seemed to speak non-stop. I remember consciously talking quickly, and not stopping, doing the same thing with a friend recently. Channeling then, I have no idea what was said.

"This is something that I will require. This is something that the body will adjust to in time."

"This is something that the body never adjusts to in time," ego pipes in.

Laughing now, I think the body doesn't adjust to it in time but somehow the process becomes easier with practice. For now, I continue to channel the unseen.

"That's not a process. It's a communication. It's a knowing to spread to the world, spread out into the world, into the Light for the rest, for them to see though the fog, because the fog is heavy now. It must be lifted. The veil must be lifted. The fog must be gone. People must be able to see that there is nothing here. There is nothing worthwhile. There is nothing worth staying for. There is nothing here.

"We all must go back to the One. It doesn't mean that there should be mass suicide, oh, heavens no. Oh, heavens no, no suicide; no, only in mind, only in mind return to the One. Only in mind return to the One. And help one another relate to the One for that is all there is. That is all there is.

There is just the One. There is only the One, only One in which we live, and breathe, and have all being. That is the one for which we seek. That is the One of which we know. That is the One that goes before us and paves the way. And brings the Light into all the spaces, all the crevices, all the creeks, every part of the world. The failsafe of all nature, of all BEing; one Being, and so it is until the end. It is just One. It is just One."

:-)

"The importance is on getting back to the Light and you can only say that as an enlightened being.

"You must be generous with what you have. God has given it to you to be generous with. There is no need for it in other worlds. Soon there will be no need for it here. The money is the important thing to give at this time. The need for it is lessening as time goes by. You will see that the barter system is the way to live on this earth and the barter system is the way this world is going. Do you understand that nothing is real in this world?"

"Yes," I reply. "Yes, I do."

"Then why do you cling to these worldly possessions?"

"I didn't think that I was clinging. I just thought I was holding on to what I might need in the future."

"God is the only Source. God is the only need. There is no need to cling to what is not real. That is your lesson for today. Situations will arise dedicated to giving. You will know when the time is ripe for giving. We are with you always. Do not be fearful. Do not be afraid for we are a part of you. And yet, nothing in this world exists wholly, freely, without the Lord."

It is now 9:10 AM on New Year's Day 2009. I was waking from a dream when the words came. Waking more fully, I grabbed the tape recorder and began to repeat the words asking the entity to stay so I could grasp them all. I did not get it all but just the gist of it. My body was hot as words came but then started to get cold when the words stopped and the entity left. This usual thing occurs when a communication comes.

Blue orbs floated, in the middle of my closed eye vision, as the entity spoke. They were violet-blue globs of light that came from the top and moved down to the bottom, one after the other, as the words filled my brain.

:-)

"Simple exercises keep positive thoughts. Know the Truth is within you. The Light shines forth if you allow it. Maintain your equilibrium through Nature. Never be one without the One within. Know ye are watched and oh so carefully loved.

"You are coming to a place in the process where all will be known to you soon. And you must listen to the direction within. Do you understand?"

"Oh yes," I announce into the recorder after repeating the words. "I understand."

"That is all that we have to relay for now. Peace be with you. Harmony abounds. Love prevails. It is done."

:-)

"We are here to support the people in their flight. There is none other to relate this particular information. All are given their freedom of choice. All are on their path now. All are participating whether they know or not.

"The time is right for seclusion. Be aware, seclusion is necessary. It is a part of the process. Do not dismay in this process, the gathering of minds. All shall know the power and the glory of the Lord. All shall know the truth will be told, in bits and pieces, wherefore it is known by all.

"The charge is great. Your plights are few. The rays to come will censure you. Fear is unknown in you. Your job is well done. Don't be alarmed at what you see, at what you hear, at what you do, for all is in perfect, Divine Order. Know that this peace is everlasting within you. Know that this love abides within you. Know that the Truth is setting you free. Know this and ye shall be safe in the ways of the Lord.

"Don't flutter about like a bee. All that you see and all that you do is divinely guided. Feel secure in the ways of the Lord for they will comfort you in the days ahead. You must commence so all will know the power and the glory of the kings. You are the glory of the Lord. Seek not to replace him for thine is the kingdom of heaven, the power and glory.

"All withstands the pressures of the earth as it comes forth in its efforts to expel the evil that has been done. Know this and be safe in the bosom of the Lord. Know this, and be secure in the knowledge, all is One, perfect, unerring One. Know this knowledge and do not be alarmed. All is well within your world.

"The plan to carry forth is occurring now. It must be entered by June of 2009. It will cause many years of changes. These changes are necessary. As *It* spews forth from the bosom of *Its* being, do not be alarmed, for all is well within your world for your world is not here.

"Trust in the Lord. The vision that you have created will subside in time. All will wholly return to the Lord. Know your heart's path is true in the Lord."

This message came during the time I studied *A Course in Miracles*. Sometimes messages hold metaphoric meanings. As I understand this message now, it is clear to me that we humans are unique parts of Consciousness. As parts of Consciousness, we designed, and continue to manifest, a world where some give their power away to others. Many are beginning to realize that we are the ones we have been waiting for. All the power we need lies within the core of our being. It is time to realize we are all those Beings we gave our power to, whether they be the Lord, God, Buddha or Hitler, all are parts of the Consciousness in which we live, and move, and have all BEing.

It is time to take back our powers of manifestation and realize there is nothing outside of Consciousness. Consciousness is one, perfect and unerring *Truth*. It's just that we forgot this and now we are part of the plan to remember.

:-)

Sometimes I get messages for others. One such communication came on March 5, 2009 for my good friend, Michael the acupuncturist. Doctor's recently diagnosed Michael's wife with breast cancer. She had the surgery and some radiation treatment. But they refused chemotherapy, opting instead to continue less invasive methods that build, instead of destroy, the immune system. The messages came for them before opening my eyes upon waking.

"There are always circumstances that seem beyond our control that pause us. We must define these circumstances in terms of living, in terms of how we wish to live. These circumstances are easily recognized as we concentrate on the higher aspects of our BEing.

"There are always circumstances that seem beyond our control in this illusion. These circumstances are not necessarily what they seem. There are ways to rid ourselves of these circumstances, and we must follow the tried, and true, method to do so. This method is the way we come back to the One, realizing that there is no limitation. That all are One, that we have never left, and shall always remain, in the bosom of the Lord. These friendly reminders help us to believe what is true.

"There are other ways to clear the emotions of dis-ease. These ways help us in becoming more alive with Source. These ways are the tried and true methods of the Masters. These emotional beliefs are not real. They don't fit into the mold. They are not a part of our natural self, for emotion is in itself human and we are not human. To let bygones be bygones is a source of Truth. Follow the path of wisdom to the Master within. That is the truth of the nature of our BEing. That is the truth of the nature of *All*.

"Relinquish the past, forget the future. Live in the Now, knowing the Now moment is the only true moment. This will carry you through. This will secure you in the life you wish to live."

:-)

Ornaments kept falling off the Christmas tree to wake me so I'd remember dreams. Now I'm told that it's possible to consciously, as I dream, change those dreams and go further than before. Although the dreams are not necessarily dreams of limitation, I can still make them better.

:-)

"You have to go forward. Stop looking for things outside yourself. All is known, all is here, all is now. Envision it. Believe it. It is the very truth of you, the heart and soul, as you would say. Stop believing in things outside yourself. That is all there is to say."

:-)

On New Year's Eve 2009, I returned from three tiresome hours of shopping with family for Momma's eightieth birthday party. When I got home, I cleared my body of caustic negative energy, by grounding to the earth, but still felt the need to shower with sea salt. After spending thirty minutes in the shower, I'm ready to work on the third book. Thoughts of automatic writing enter my mind when the

Microsoft Word program starts unexpectedly. It's something I've tried before with some success. My fingers move swiftly over the keyboard.

"So now I will type a message for you. It will be sweet and to the point. Listen well as I tell you what not to do, for you are one with *All*, and it does not matter what you do here. Do you hear what I say? It does not matter what you do here but let all actions speak of love, for love is all there is, even if you don't think so.

"Take for instance, the situation you seem to be in. It is not existent. It is not worthy of your or anyone's consideration. You must turn to the path of Light and Truth in all circumstances and turn the other cheek. The energy you share is rewarded hereafter and forevermore.

"Seek not to displeasure others for it is only yourself you displeasure. The truth needs to be known by all and you can do that with your writing but you must do it gently and wholly. Turn the other cheek and let it slide past. Let it slide past you. Focus instead on the truth of your BEing as One, for the Light is within you, and you know that to be true.

"Save others if you wish, but recall you are here, separate, but in Truth One. What one does here is non-consequential as far as the truth goes here, for there is NO Truth here. What cannot be understood here is enlightened on the other side of the Truth. For all is darkness here and the scale of truth leads to Light quickly once you transcend the path before you.

"Move quickly now and transcend that path wholly, completely, and forevermore. It is all there is to say. Do it now. Don't burden yourself with physical matters for they are just that, physical, and nothing physical is real.

"Go, go forth, and spread the word. The Truth is known to few but increases in the Light of God. Your BEing is one in Truth that is all you need to know."

:-)

Curse words enter my brain while sleeping. I wake to ask how the human heart protects me. A message comes minutes later.

"A material heart protects me from harm, shimmering ever so slightly with wavering light."

:-)

Well, another amazing thing just happened. I was awake and aware, lying with closed eyes while with two Beings. One said something to the other about preparing me to receive more energy, to prepare two points so I could accept more energy. I sensed they were my third eye and crown chakra and immediately thought, "Well let me position my body first." A pillow sat under my thighs as I lay on my back and I was going to adjust it to be more comfortable. My arms were at my side.

All of the sudden, I couldn't move. My body was paralyzed, then levitated and, it seemed, plugged into a light socket. "Was I going to fly around the room?" I thought, as my body lifted off the bed. It hovered about two inches off the mattress and shook from head to toes. It was as if something plugged me into a light socket as my body intensely vibrated. I was aware of a triangle-shaped light in my third eye for a few fleeting seconds before my body stopped vibrating and returned to rest on the bed. The entire event lasted for probably less than a minute.

Gratefulness filled me knowing that my body received more Light, more of the Light of what we are because we are really, literally, Light. We've just come here to play a game and now it's time to return back to the One. It's time to return back to Light. This time, we're doing it while still in the human body. I'm grateful to be one of the illusionary souls who volunteered to show the others that it can be done.

:-)

"It is time to concentrate on the big picture of Reality. All things fall away in the true scheme of things. The meaning on this road never ends because it is an illusionary road we call life. The road is in our mind. You're going to go the distance this time. You're home free. In these trying times, the key is faith. Faith is the key to all things."

Lightning flashes in the distance as the all too familiar wave of exhaustion overwhelms me. Sleep soon offers a refuge from the muscle aches and tiredness but I wake within the hour with an ache in my temporal lobe. Once again, my throat feels like sandpaper until I drink water from the bottle on my nightstand. Gripping walls to steady myself, I make my way to the bathroom. This type of activity is now normal upon waking during the night for I'm still wobbling between dimensions.

After waking several times over the course of a few hours, it's clear that other energies are refining the new human template. A message breaks through the lightning and rain.

"It is time dear One. It is time to merge, to merge back with the One in which you live. In the Whole you are free to grow, to expand, to enrich all around you. Merge with the One. Know you are Light. Know you are the Wind. Merge with the One knowing all is well. Merge with the Good. Merge with the Love. Merge with the Light knowing all is well."

The usual heat saturates my body. I lay spread-eagle upon the bed anchoring myself with one hand facing up and the other palm down. My heart pounds in tune to the slight throb in my head. It seems easy to merge as a sense of lightness fills me from head to toe. I merge with the surrounding air for several minutes before drifting back to sleep.

The sun seems to have disappeared from the sky now. Storms continue to surround the area in which I reside. It's raining again. Thunder echoes all around. Yet, I know that the paradise where we live as One remains secure. That place becomes closer to our reality each day. Expand your energy field and merge with the One to feel it.

:-)

Music from the multiple-disc CD player begins to play erratically as I type into the old laptop while working on the fourth book in 2010. I stop typing to listen and sure enough, a message comes.

"Get ready. Get ready for the big one, as you say, for there will be some widespread noise here on earth within the next few days. Do not let it alarm you for all is well. All is in Divine Order. It is only a mere inconvenience for some but devastating to others. Take care in the days ahead and stay strong, seek not outside yourself for you know where the real world is. All is well. Don't buy into the fear."

:-)

After years of strongly sensing Daniel's presence, and hearing a non-stop flow of words enter my brain, it seems hard to become accustomed to channeling True Self without it. I now find myself asking for confirmation that this isn't my own ego trying to take control once again.

"These words are not out of the ordinary like before," I find myself saying. "I'm not hearing an unfamiliar string of words. These words sound like something I'd say myself."

"Ah Mom, aren't you listening?" Daniel says. "It's all you. Each day it becomes more you. You've got to listen. Things can never be back the way they were. Those words won't flow into your head the way they used to because it's all you. You're the only one. Those words come forth from your heart. Those words come forth, not from the brain, but from the heart, the heart of God. Know this to be true."

Karen Drucker's "Hold on to Love" plays in the background as Daniel's essence continues. Conscious control of my breath abruptly disappears as it quickens.

"The heart of God is everlasting. The heart of God never ends. The heart of God goes on and on forevermore. You are within the heart of God and the heart of God is expanding, expanding to cover the universe, this world, and all the worlds within the One, within the One that all live. Allow the heart to expand."

I now set the voice activation on my tape recorder in readiness for another message.

"Get used to these energies Mom. Flow with them. Quit fighting them. Quit going back into yourself. Expand, that's why you're watching all these things, all these people that tell you to expand. You need to stop pulling back. You need to stop extracting parts of yourself and expand."

The CD player continues to pause and restart haphazardly as his words flow through my brain. My throat is now dry and I feel the force of his energy field surrounding me.

:-)

"In the end, loving kindness paves the way to the Truth of the Presence within you. The Truth of the Presence is within you."

I begin to fall asleep but again speak into the tape recorder now lying next to my head.

"We are the voice for the Truth of the Presence. The Truth of the Presence is within you. Every act of loving kindness paves the way to the Truth of the Presence within you. All things known to man will change. The old fades, the old fades quickly away as the new takes its place. The Truth of

LightworkersLog.com

the Presence is known within. The Truth of the Presence is known within everything.

"Go forth and spread the word of the Truth of this Presence. It's in everything, for it is the only Truth there is. All else shall fade quickly away as the new encompasses the old. The Truth of this Presence within you is everlasting. We are one voice speaking for the Truth of the Presence.

"Stay clear of the chaos around you. It will not affect you but it will be everywhere. Stay focused on the Voice of the Presence within. Know that this is the only Truth. The Light you hold within is everlasting and it is within all living things. This Light shall shine brightly in the days to come but you must be careful to guard that Light.

"The Voice of the Presence is within and is served by your greatness. Do not be dissuaded by the voice of others for it is the Voice within that is the Truth. Know this and be not afraid in the days to come. Listen and speak the Voice of Truth. You are one of many speaking this Voice, knowing this Truth. You are not alone, despite your physical location. Know that all is well in the days to come and serve the Voice of Truth, with honor, with justice, with love, knowing that all is well.

"The end of the old is very near. The new shall flood the world of woe and wash all those ways away. The darkness comes quickly and leaves an everlasting mark upon the face of the earth. Hear the ways of the Voice and know that all is well. Listen, listen within, that is the only task you are given."

:-)

Automatic writing consciously begins with this:

"There are so many things I can feed with my energy, so many things I could tell you, but I now choose my vocalizations carefully. I know now that everything I think or talk about feeds it energy. We are in a time of great change and you can be a part of this change.

"Consider your actions and words. Consider if you want to continue living the life you live. It is a choice regardless of what you believe. It is a choice to live in poverty. It is a choice to live in pain. You must reconsider these choices and think again. Is this what you want for your life? Do you really want to suffer now that you know it is unnecessary?

"The vast choices before you are beautifully perfect in all things. You can live the life you wish for now the world is your oyster. Choose your thoughts carefully for soon what you wish for will manifest much quicker than ever before. We are in the end of the old ways, the end of humanity's sleep. Listen. Take the time to listen to the Voice within you for it is ever speaking. Know that this is the true voice of humanity for God is truly all there is. Go forth and spread the word of One."

:-)

There was a time, not too long ago, when I stopped frequently to bless people met along this road of life. I don't do that very much now and yet know it is a necessary thing to speed our progression back to Truth. The truth is we are spiritual beings living a dualistic life on earth. For many of us it is now time to return to the Light of our true BEing, the Light of One. After all, it is where we have come from and where all will return.

Many people are now preparing to leave this planet, including some of my family members. It's not easy to stand by knowing this truth so I asked for something to help them pass quickly into the Light. "A Blessing of One" flowed through as I asked for guidance. At first, it did not make much sense but now I see it makes perfect sense. We are the result of our thought here on earth but in *Truth* One.

"I offer a blessing for those now in the transition between duality and wholeness. It spreads throughout the land of woe, which seems to cover the planet of earth.

"It is not a likely thing to let go of duality while still in human form but this blessing will assist in processing those who wish to help others do so. It is not a blessing that comes from this human host but rather one that comes from the core of BEing, the core of our soul, the Truth of One. Unto itself it is not needed, and never will be, but to the human it is wholly needed during these times of vast change.

"We as humans are making our way ever so slowly and carefully back to whole freedom of Self. This Self is what we are, and yet, it too is imagined in our host of Hosts.

"And so the blessing begins.

"Follow me now to Truth, to Light, to Wholeness and Love. Follow me to the very core issues that stop humanity from progressing and now to the Light I offer a Oneness host.

"The Light fills all of humanity with it's brilliance. It fills every spot seen and unseen. It controls all issues of light and dark and relentlessly follows the path back to Oneness. It is the enlightenment of people everywhere for now the Truth has entered the realm of many to bless, to own, to the Truth of One.

"I bless all seen and unseen, all left and forgotten, all here but never here, with the Light of One. It is the Light of Truth to carry those of you Home who wish to leave now as the games continue relentlessly.

"Know that there is nothing to stop you from leaving this planet to return to Light. Know that the truth of your being, the truth of all beings, is One everlasting, grateful One.

"Fill all with the security of Oneness and within that Oneness there is the most brilliant Light to help all who waver along the path. The Truth of BEing is known to few but shall spread quickly, ever so quickly, to One."

:-)

"Please be aware that the earth is changing rapidly and the body within changes as well. Know that all is well within the soul of One for that never changes. Peace is always with you, above and below, within and without.
"You are the thought that builds the world, the image that radiates the Light. Be careful with those thoughts and words. It is time to get together; focus as One more clearly. It is time to come together and shine your Light. The brilliance of that Light is everlasting. It shines across the land purifying and cleansing all. Just as you trust in the future of humanity as One, you must trust in the Power within. Know that Power is within you and bear the Light wherever you go consciously spreading it across the land. Know the land is your sacred home."

I recall dreaming of a group of Lightworkers coming together for a meeting of like-minds right before this message came. Many Lightworkers now come forward to form local groups. These Lightworkers stopped looking outside themselves. They are unlikely to frequent places of worship or centers of learning. They value and nurture a knowing that comes from direct experience of the One in which we live, and move, and have all BEing. They don't push their knowledge on others but offer it freely when approached. Their time is best spent consciously radiating the Light into everyone and everything. If you are in this state of awareness, consider forming a Lightworker support group in your area.

:-)

The world is changing at an alarming rate. High solar activity resulted in a series of coronal mass ejections affecting earth during February 2011. A new sunspot emerged quickly to become wider than the planet Jupiter unleashing the strongest solar flares since December 2006. NASA's Solar Dynamics Observatory recorded intense flashes of extreme ultraviolet radiation while brief radio blackouts occurred. Major solar flares continue to erupt on the sun and as they do, the messages I hear increase. These seem to fit together.

"It is a matter of resonating with the One. You either resonate with the One now, or resonate with the One later. There is no if. It is a matter of resonating with the one Light of all BEing."

"We seek to return to the Light, and yet, there is no returning for the Light resides inside each and every one of us. That Light is everlasting, and if we choose, we can tap into that Light, very easily, and very efficiently. Knowing that all come together as Light in the end of what you call your world, there is no end and no beginning. There is only one pure and brilliant Light to resonate with, to be, to shine. Resonate with the one Light knowing, as you do, you resonate with the One of *All*."

:-)

Allow me to address the subject of karma. Many people seem to be going through circumstances, which seem beyond their control at this time. These things are not beyond their control, for again, everything is truly in our mind. We mold this world with our thought. It's important to realize this if one is struggling, with situations that seem beyond their control because of others.

We come into this world as souls seeking, most of us, seeking to balance the karma created long ago. And yet, karma is just another thing in the illusion. We need not struggle. We need not continue to stay in a situation that no longer serves us. We need only to be true to our self, that one lovely Self of *All*. It is the only truth that there is. The one Self serves all for we are each a part of the one Self.

There is no not knowing this one Self. It is just a matter of recognizing and tapping in. And so, if you are one of those struggling in a situation that seems beyond your control think of changing your situation through the power of thought. Position yourself in a place where you have only positive interactions with yourself and others. You do this by maintaining positive thoughts.

Turn off your televisions. Turn off your radios. Stop reading the news. These things only serve to keep you in the negativity of this dream. You can create your own positive dream by focusing only on positive things. I've done it. I know it can be done.

Karma is a game of balance we choose to play when we come here. And if situations don't improve, despite everything, every effort we have made, we don't need to continue to suffer. We need only to make the best possible effort to keep things positive in our own mind.

:-)

As with many things, the task I sought to complete today turned out to be a guided task of service to One. My fingertips are now sore from pounding at the keys, without rest. When messages come though, they do so in a steady stream of words that fill my brain, and it is awfully hard to document them.

Sometimes I ask for the words to slow down, so I can keep up, but the process always goes very quickly. I mentally take note of changes that may need to occur in grammar and spelling, as I type, and then make those corrections when the energy dissipates. In any event, here is the message received minutes ago. I trust you will relate to it as well.

"The world is changing quickly and you are changing ever more quickly. Thank you for allowing yourself to grow by ridding yourself of past trauma. You know it is necessary to do so to continue on at the great rate you now find yourself in. Do not be dismayed by the fast progress, or the slow progress of others, for you must realize it is all really just you. You are a Being of Light who has chosen to experience this as quickly as possible to get back to the One of *All*.

"Concern yourself with nothing of this world for the world continues to drastically change, as you stand by, not knowing what is up or down. Do not let the dribbles of time affect your vibration, for that is what will carry you Home, quicker than the blink of an eye. Be sorry for nothing, and no one, and remember this is but a dream, a poorly planned dream of nothingness, and despair, for many who care to indulge in the senses of the little mind.

"You are free to do as you please, and recall please, that you are being watched over and cared for by Beings, not of this illusionary world, and yet we too are illusion. There is no dark where the Light shines and know that you and others hold that Light ever so brightly now.

"Be truthful to your Source of One and know all is going according to plan, the Divine Plan of One, to return the many fragments back to Wholeness. It is a necessary process that will quell the heart of many savage beasts. Beware nothing and fear not in the days ahead. Know all is well and shall be forevermore to those who hold the Light of One.

"Speak not of separation for naught does it serve you. A knowingness comes to the many soon so prepare to teach the Law of One. You and many others will serve in this role of Light. Know this and be assured as you move along the path to Home. All is well and can be nothing else."

:-)

Words come to me on April 18, 2011, as I lie between waking and sleep in the wee hours of the morning.

"It is with the greatest of honor that I perceive through the veil of illusion."

:-)

When words come easily into my brain as I lie in the state between waking and sleep, I play attention to them, especially today on August 5, 2011. This morning's words did not seem to come from the now familiar place, which I refer to as Inner Speak. And yet, I know *All That Is* is One and it is within me.

I do not watch television or read the newspaper, and rarely, except to check weather and other earth changes, follow Internet links. Frankly, I am not sure how this message came to me. It mentions the name of a Being and a planet that I have not heard about. However, the messenger seemed very loving and I am not in the habit of receiving communications from negative entities.

A strong belief in *All That Is*, which we each savor as a Divine Spark within our heart's core, permeates both days and nights. And yet, while I still seem to be in a physical body it seems prudent to document and share messages.

So now, at six-thirty in the morning, hours before my usual rising time, I document the words that flowed so easily minutes ago.

"I am Talia from the planet Nibiru. I wish to speak with you today. Your planet is wholesome in many ways. Today is a day of great opportunities. Shine forth the Light to see them all. Manifesting your dreams is easier now as these great changes take place. Be aware that with each change in your earth the space for new beginnings opens wider.

"The land of your ancestors opens to you for your grace. There is a great cataclysm taking place in your atmosphere that opens the way for new beginnings. Do not be afraid as these necessary changes take place. All is according to the Divine Will of One. Take care in the days ahead and know all is as it should be for the further evolution of humanity.

"Reap not in sorrow or haste but take each change with the Wholeness and Love that you are."

:-)

"It is an unprecedented event."

The words run though my brain on the cusp of sleep. I immediately wake to ask, "What is?"

"The changing of the world view."

:-)

My companions now appear more often to let me know I'm not alone. After seeing more of the beloved tiny, white lights, words fill my brain.

"Know that the process is almost complete. Fear not as we move forward."

:-)

Thanksgiving Day, 2011

"Just know you're not alone, not really. I know you are accustomed to being with the family on holidays, such as today, but just know that all is in Divine Order. Sometimes you have to let go to grow. You know that but others may not so just let go and let them grow. It will all become increasingly clear as the day goes on that separation in mind is not the way to exist on any level. Know this in your heart, your mind.

"Your soul speaks of a time long ago when our essence was untainted by the ways of this world. It is time to remember that time of innocence. What comes into your life now is full of the good that is and will always be. Just know that all is in Divine Order.

"Are you done working the ways of the world? You see how erratic they can be when working with unseen energies for even as you type the words flow erratically about the screen. It is better to use the old ways of listening and recording and then transcribing if you wish to avoid this.

"I love you Mom just know that I'm always with you. We are all here for we are a part of one another and that is becoming increasingly clear to you as the old world falls away. Hang in there and know you are not working alone. We work beside you as representatives of the One that truly is."

Apparently, the field of energy within me strengthened today. This was the first message that was hard to type into the new computer for the text kept jumping around, leaving parts of words on different lines. And now, as I edit this book it continues to do so, very often, making documentation cumbersome.

:-)

Thanksgiving Night

"You must stop relating to these world events for they are not of your true nature. Think, and report, only on the good of *All There Is* for that is now your charge here. Do not dwell upon the other side of life that you have left far behind. Listen for the wisdom you hold inside you and know all is, and continues to be, going according to the grand scheme of things.
"It is all moving very quickly now and soon you will be settled in your new home with your new friends, all of like-mind. Fear not, for all is going according to plan and soon this old way will fade away. Do not be concerned with what you are leaving behind because there is no behind in this or any world. The world you see is an illusion of your own making and you must concentrate more on building a new world of Love and Light and Good, regardless of the chaos around the physical form. Stay still and listen to the still Voice within and know all is well in your world. That's it. That's all for now."

:-)

Words began to fill my head, this morning on December 12, 2011, before rising. They came after a few bouts of unexpected, but familiar, breathing, where I re-activate the

Light within, with ease and grace. Still filled with the sleep of a human, I decided to sit later in the day to receive a message. I thought about telling everyone how we are reactivating more Light to hold within. And then the message began…

"I will never be that upon which things happen. I will continue to manifest my own world of wonder, of love, of glory, of abundance and Truth. The *That* of which I AM is limitless, Truth, abiding in the ethers of non-space and non-local reality. And the *That* of which I AM is ready to return to the wholeness of One. I abide in the *All That Is* now and forevermore. And knowing this Truth, I AM free of the constraints of this world.

"Repeat after me:

"I AM free, a sovereign Being living in the Light of Love. There is none other but the *All That Is* of which I AM. A part of wholeness and Truth ever-abides in this BEing of Greatness. *All That Is* is the very core of all things and all that is and ever will be. The Truth abides in all to see, to hear, to know. Feel it within you now and know that all is very, very well as we move forward on this Mother Earth Ship."

More words come many minutes later after resting.

"Grateful I AM to be a sovereign Being ever present in the Light of One."

:-)

Words come after breathing in through the nose and out through the mouth to continue reactivating the Light within.

"We come together to help the people of earth. It is our supreme wish, desire, to do so. All is illusion for there is no earth. And yet, we know, to those minds lost in the maze, it seems so very real. Know that all is going according to the Divine Plan as you move further into this illusion of power versus Love. Love, has and always, will survive. We are with you every step of the way. Do not fear."

:-)

Before rising on the morning of December 21, 2011, I note a memo into the recorder. "Write an article on preparing for uncertainties (stocking up on food and water), the importance of going within, and deciding what your role is and playing it." In the afternoon as I sit ready to write, the following words flow quickly through me.

"As long as we remain encased in a body, it seems prudent to make the world a better place. We do this by changing the way we manifest, by looking at things in new ways and adding positive spins to all that occurs.

"For instance, let's say you lost your job. On one hand, it would seem devastating to not have a steady income. But on another, it opens a whole new world of possibilities. These possibilities existed before the job loss but are now enhanced in your mind because of the job loss. So what are these possibilities? For one, you have the opportunity to do as you please, to find your passion, and start a new way of living.

"Perhaps you didn't know how to exist without having a steady place to visit during the day but now you are on to another whole new level of understanding. You know the day starts in your mind. It is not based upon a timepiece or 'bosses law' but starts with the value of your memory to call it what you will.

"Do not be so distant to new thoughts for they will take you into another realm of existence, within your mind, that never leaves you feeling empty. The point of this speech

LightworkersLog.com

is to give you new ways to think, new ideas, new ways to manifest by envisioning what your heart's desire is.

"Think of a time when you existed solely to BE. That time is quickly returning now and you hold the key as to when it occurs. All those on the path of One share that key. Knowing all is one significant, vast state of BEing should help to secure the future you seek. This future does not rely upon a job, a home, or even the people we currently see. It evolves around your thoughts, your ability to manifest and dream a new dream of truth, of light, of wholeness and health.

"The prosperity you seek is already yours. You need only believe in the Source of One to manifest that new dream now. The answers you seek are within you. Do not be dissuaded by the mass consciousness that appears outside of you. This is only a ploy to keep you in the dream of limitation. Seek nothing outside yourself. Learn to trust in the wholeness of *All That Is* to meet your everyday needs."

:-)

Admittedly, I still waver between trusting and wondering if the messages that come though me are valid points of consideration. A thought wakes me on December 28, 2011 at 4:42 AM.

"Everything here is energy."

Nothing is solid. Humanity constantly deals with energy from all sorts of sources. Some are synthetic such as television and radio while other sources are what we refer to as natural, such as geomagnetic waves.

Thoughts are energy. These thoughts go throughout all the space that we live in. If we sequester ourselves, we deal mainly with our own thoughts. But the more we go out into the world, the more people we are around, the more thoughts we have to deal with because everything is energy.

Wind and rain carry thoughts. When the wind strengthens or it rains, the energy gets denser. And messages seem to increase when the sun erupts.

"Thoughts become young and steadily increase through the mind of One when spoken. All thoughts energize in the consciousness in which you live. All thoughts become manifestation by which you live."

:-)

Thoughts enter my brain while waking in the wee hours of the morning.

"So, in my world everything is a part of me. There is no separation. And yet, things appear so distinctly outside my Self of One. What things must I concentrate on to nurture this Self of One? Of utmost importance is reactivation of the Light within. That alone is my primary responsibility. Aside from that, ego seems to rule. It must be acknowledged that there is no, nor was there ever, separation. All the things that my Self of One concentrates on are really things to clear, to purify, to release from thoughts of separation."

"You now see how that limits the possibilities of egos domain. As things fall away from your life it becomes increasingly clear that all things are, were, just figments of imagination. Since you have cleansed and purified these thought forms, released them back into the ether of One to further expand, the field is wide open to manifest the New World. The thoughts before you now are of peace, wholeness, and the Light that you truly are.

"Take nothing for granted in the coming days. But know you hold the key to humanities happiness, wholeness, and truth in your Self of One. Remember, there is nothing outside that Self of One. What you relate to clues you into what you need to improve, in the expansion of thought, within your Self of One. In other words, the things that

LightworkersLog.com

remain in your mind, in your consciousness, are the things to concentrate on.

"Do they speak of Oneness or separation? If they speak of separation, that is what the world will continually present. When this occurs, remember to purify, cleanse, and forgive the mis-thought. This alone will serve to lift the Self of One to further wholeness. Lest you forget, in the Self of One's world you have never really left the Whole. It is only in the thought form of physicality that separation exists. Be aware that the game continues to change. But all is well for the Self of One that concentrates solely on the Oneness of *Truth*."

:-)

In late January 2012, I lie in bed waiting for the energies within to dissipate. Recognition of these energies started a few years ago when it felt like atoms were bouncing within the confines of my form. Now the energies are much more intense, more densely packed, and more structured, but I am handling them much better. A message comes as I wonder whether to go back to sleep as usual.

"You are going to have to find a way to deal with these energies for this vibration is what you will feel more so in the days to come."

These stronger energies are apparently normal when the physical bodies' vibration increases so I have to get used to it. Hopefully, the ringing in my ears will dissipate in time.

:-)

"All things come in time. Thus sayeth the Lord of your imaginary heart. And yet, as you know, all earth life is in the image of ones small mind of One. This One, the Whole of many ones, as yet unknown to all humanity on a greater level, is but the inkling of knowledge that exists.

LightworkersLog.com

"Times in your world now quickly, very quickly, morph to a somewhat decayed state of awareness for many who do not follow the path of *Truth*. Know that in the true Reality all things remain unchanged.

"Do not be dissuaded by the masses, which cry out for help outside of their small self. Those in tune with *All That Is* know of the Power they hold within to change awareness into a true state of bliss, despite surrounding circumstances. Know that all things change in your world to bring all to the greater state of awareness that there is nothing outside the small self."

For those wondering how these messages come to me, let me enlighten you by noting I do not usually seek them out. Most messages come while I am involved in the mundane tasks of life while listening to music. Some messages come on the cusp of sleep while others flow into my brain when I tune in after becoming aware of a change in how music plays on the CD player. This message flowed from head to hand after one word repeated while a CD of my favorite songs played.

:-)

"Listen to thy truth within the core of BEing. It is the only Truth to hearken forth remedies of thought not of your making. These are ageless truths merely unknown to the mind of ego and yet known as *All* to the Mind of One. Come forth in all your glory to relish in the Light of One, for reality seeps even closer to the depths of your innocent being. The days of yore, unspoken of in outer circles, knows nothing of the untold truths of yesteryear."

I listen as the CD player continues to malfunction. It's annoying, to say the least, as I wait for words to ceaselessly flow again.

"An ever present BEing exists on all levels but is not easily tapped into due to restraints forced upon those on earth.

These restraints will soon be lifted entirely and all who care to listen will hear the Truth of One. In no way, shape, or form, is this occurring on the cabals watch, and yet, there is only the cabal in the little mind of ego. There is a sense of Oneness that permeates all of this, and every, planet now as the alignment continues to move closer to Truth.

"In this space of evolutionary time, all is known and yet all is forsaken in the realms of darkness. Let it not dissuade you from knowing the Light of One exists within, in a place where it is safe and secure. There is nothing and no one that can delete this space for its secureness reaches out into the vast beyond.

"All is coming closer to an end of darkness as we beckon forth the forces necessary to bring in more and more Light to earth. The spaces of Mother Earth are filling quickly with this Light of One. Be not afraid as these changes take place but know all is well within the scope of non-limitation, unerringly perfect and already complete."

I wish to type a few more words as the CD continues to jolt the music, rather erratically, to stop it from playing normally. And yet, this occurrence is again something new to me. It's not acting as other times but playing, stopping, and then seeming to quiver as I wait for more words.

Will I finish the fourth book in my series as a "soap opera segment" or finish the *Book of One :-)*?

:-)

Today would have been Daniel's forty-fourth birthday. As I write listening to Daniel Namod sing "One Power" in the background, the music begins to waver. The spirit of my last-born son fills the air as his words enter my head. I type furiously to get them all before they disappear.

"I love you Mom even when I know you don't believe I am here. I am always with you, always. Don't forget that as we move forward in time to its end. All is well in your world and will become increasingly so. So don't sweat the small stuff. I knew you'd like that. It is a favorite saying of mine right before I went Home to rest a bit. It is so awesome over there in Mind, the big Mind, not the little one that we seem to relish in.

"Stay clear of the drama Ma for you know it will only pull you back into the maze. Stay out of the drama and know that all is well as we move forward through this time of great change. All is well and will continue to be. Don't fret. It does not serve you well. Smile more, go out more, move more, be more. Continue to strive for more of the real you, that one that does not want material things but just to BE. Just to BE is the only thing worthy of your time. Don't forget that it will always be there for you to play with.

"I know things may not appear wholesome at times but you must move forward out of the maze to the true Reality of One. It is an everlasting place of wholeness and truth, the only place of consequence. BE, just BE for the sake of BEing and know that all is well.

"You ask about the books now. It is your charge to write them. Your souls charge but you know there is no soul, no body, no impermanance. So now, you do what occupies your time. But yet, it seems to serve the masses, which seem outside you. Remember, nothing is outside you, or anyone, for there is in Reality only One. That is the key to living. There is only One in which all reside. Living that truth by just BEing is crucial in other realms of Reality, which you shall soon see for yourself. Take everything in stride and know that all is very, very well in your world and your world is the only world there is."

Tidbits on BEing

What if life on earth was an illusion in states of awareness? What if our emotions contributed to the length of our stay? What would happen if we stopped playing the game? What would happen if we stopped being emotional? What would happen if we stopped being so 'mental' thinking we had to figure things out? What would happen if we decided to just BE?

What does it mean to just BE? It means to just live in the Now moment. It means to stop trying to figure things out. It means to stop thinking about changing lives that never were. It means to stop visiting the astral world, the other worlds in which we think we live.

BEing is a new state of awareness. BEing, just BEing, is a state of One. It is living in the Now. It is enjoying the moment. It is forgetting there ever was a past, nor will there ever be a future. BEing is Now. BEing is our natural state.

What if the natural state of BEing is to experience, to express, and to expand through loving acts of kindness?

"It is always advantageous for the soul to grow, to experience new things. Don't worry so much about being stuck in the dream. Just BE. Just BE without limitation; just experience new things without remorse. Just live the love you were born to give. Expansion is in the experience of BEing."

:-)

"One does not need to study. One needs only to BE, to express the God within. Expression, expansion, experience, that is why you are here. You're here to experience and express Source. And through that experience and expression,

Source expands. That is vital to know. There is no right or wrong here. There is only expansion and expression. Again, there is no right or wrong here. There is only expansion and expression through experience, the experience of the soul. Yes, soul is an illusion as well, a required illusion for the body to experience, expand, express. We are One living in a state of grace forever. That is the truth of the matter."

About the Author

SAM is a wayshower helping others to learn the truth of their being so humanity can return to Source. She is a lifelong believer in the power of Love. Her inspiring life demonstrates the strength of Mind over matter. It is a story of progression from desperation to hope, poverty to riches, limitation to freedom, and fear to Love.

The awareness that we are spirits in human form, having a physical experience, came after SAM's son transitioned on April 4, 2004. Her quest for self-mastery began the following year when his essence led her through the doors of an establishment teaching the Science of Mind. SAM turned her back on traditional medicine after decades of illness and multiple surgeries. Using Eastern medicine, and the teachings of Ernest Holmes, she successfully rid herself of many maladies.

SAM's book series is a personal account highlighting the process of one Lightworker's awakening. Books from this author include:

Book One: Death of the Sun

Book Two: A Change in Perception

Transformation :-) Book Three

Prayer Treatments

Adventures in Greece and Turkey

Earth Angels

Return to Light :-) John of God Helps

LightworkersLog.com

Bits of Wisdom

Book of One :-) Volume 1

SAM is administrator of the popular Internet resource, Lightworker's Log (LightworkersLog.com). She currently concentrates on writing and spreading Spirit's message of Oneness throughout the globe. Guided by messages and synchronicities, SAM knows her most valuable asset is the ever-increasing awareness of our true BEing, unique figments of *All That Is*.

www.ingramcontent.com/pod-product-compliance
Lightning Source LLC
Chambersburg PA
CBHW070555050426
42450CB00011B/2880